In the northern states during the four decades after 1815, modern America was born—an enterprising but anxious America in which the capitalist ethic of gain had an impact on many people. America was rapidly expanding. To observers it appeared to promise nearly unlimited prosperity. Yet for thousands of blacks, women, children, recent immigrants, factory workers, and common laborers this promised plenty was thwarted by the daily realities of racism, sexism, poverty, and exploitation.

During these years, for the first time in the nation's history, rapid change became the norm. Industry and transportation were revolutionized. Distances shrank. Bustling crowded cities appeared. Expectations were raised and most people hoped for wealth. The more idealistic reformers came to see human perfectability as a possibility as they attacked the great problems of the period—slavery, racism, sexism, and the general misuse of persons and earth. The utopian visions of the reformers were never fully realized. But these men and women did help to shape a more humane society; their ideals still inspire.

These were exciting, formative years, and Douglas Miller's account, drawn from contemporary sources, beautifully portrays both the major themes of the age and the daily drama in the lives of ordinary people.

The Living History Library

General Editor: John Anthony Scott

THEN
WAS THE
FUTURE

The North in the Age of Jackson

1815-1850

DOUGLAS T. MILLER

Illustrated with contemporary prints and photographs

ALFRED A. KNOPF : NEW YORK

Library of Congress Cataloging in Publication Data

Miller, Douglas T. Then was the Future (The Living History Library)
Summary: Discusses the period in which the United States changed from a traditional, pre-industrial society to a modern capitalist state. Includes primary source material.

Bibliography: p. 1. United States—History—1815–1850—Juvenile literature. [1.   United States—History—1815–1850] I.   Title. E338.M62   973.5   73–5652   ISBN 0–394–82633–7 ISBN 0–394–92633–1 (lib. ed.)

For Arden and Gilman

CONTENTS

INTRODUCTION

In the Jacksonian generation Americans, as one of them noted, had stood "on the brink of fate." Would America remain an agrarian land of self-sufficient farmers and craftsmen, or would the nation be plunged into the complex world of industrial capitalism? Few persons were aware of even making a choice, but they chose nevertheless, and from the 1820s through the 1850s they revolutionized the American economy with results as significant as those stemming from their earlier political revolution. These decades were the initial era of America's modernization and as such are among the most important in the nation's history. The United States changed from a traditional preindustrial society, slow to accept innovations, to a modern capitalist state in which people believed in change and "progress."

It was in the northern states that the modern America of cities, factories, railroads, and steamboats emerged, and, although much of this book applies to the entire United States, the focus is on the North. More than any other section, the North represented America's future— a future of triumphant technology, vast wealth, and unprecedented power.

The rapidity of change was startling. For instance, a person born in New York City around 1800 would have witnessed in his lifetime such phenomenon as Fulton's first successful steamboat in 1807; the 1825 opening of the 360-mile Erie Canal; balloon flights, railroads, and transatlantic steamships in the early 1830s; the telegraph in the 1840s. During these years this individual would have seen New York grow from a small city of some 60,000 inhabitants at the beginning of the century to one of the world's major metropolises with nearly a million persons by 1860.

The speed of change helped generate great optimism. Persons came to accept improvement as the norm. While most thought of betterment in material terms, more idealistic individuals came to believe in human perfectability and organized to rid the world of war, slavery, racism, sexism, intemperance, and other evils.

Yet, if rapid changes created high hopes, they also caused conflicts and tensions. The great industrialization of the era is a good example. For some this meant vast new wealth and a higher living standard; but for thousands of workers—women, children, and immigrants particularly—the industrial revolution brought only increasingly regimented and depersonalized employment at wages that seldom reached beyond the barest subsistence.

In other instances human institutions were slow to adapt to the new realities brought about by technological changes. Politics was a case in point. The two-party system that emerged in the Jacksonian era was characterized by coalition parties seeking to win the broadest possible support. In practice this meant that basic economic, social, and moral issues were either ignored or compromised.

Therefore, politics, though covered, is not the major theme of this book. Rather I have chosen to treat the North in the age of Jackson as a totality with economic, social, intellectual, psychological, and moral realities. Modern America was born in the Jacksonian North; its birth has profoundly altered the subsequent course of America's history and the world's.

THEN
WAS THE
FUTURE

-1-

A RESTLESS, ANXIOUS PEOPLE

Life consists in motion; . . . the United States present cer-
tainly the most animated picture of universal bustle and
activity of any country in the world. Such a thing as rest or
quiescence does not even enter the mind of an American.

Francis Grund (1837)

Speaking before the delegates of the New York Con-
stitutional Convention in 1821, James Kent, a distinguished jurist, proclaimed:

We stand this moment on the brink of fate, on the
very edge of the precipice. . . . We are no longer to
remain plain and simple republics of farmers, like New-
England colonists, or the Dutch settlements on the
Hudson. We are fast becoming a great nation, with
great commerce, manufactures, population, wealth, lux-
uries, and with the vices and miseries that they engender.

Kent was testifying to the rapid growth and expansion
that was markedly altering America in the years after
1815. Many other persons also noted how new and
changed society seemed. In 1824 the renowned Massachusetts senator, Daniel Webster, stated: "Our age is

wholly of a different character, and its legislation takes another turn. Society is full of excitement."

The excitement of which Webster spoke had not abated twelve years later when he addressed the Society for the Diffusion of Useful Knowledge in Boston. On that occasion, Webster, one of the most noted orators of the age, addressed himself to the question of change and its causes.

There has been in the course of half a century an unprecedented augmentation of general wealth. Even within a shorter period, and under the actual observation of most of us, in our own country and our own circles, vastly increased comforts have come to be enjoyed by the industrious classes, and vastly more leisure and time are found for the cultivation of the mind. . . . This is a truth so evident and so open to common observation as matter of fact, that proof by particular enumeration of circumstances becomes unnecessary. We may safely take the fact to be, as it certainly is, that there are certain causes which have acted with peculiar energy in our generation, and which have improved the condition of the mass of society with a degree of rapidity heretofore altogether unknown.

What, then, are these causes? This is an interesting question. It seems to me the main cause is the successful application of science to art.

Webster went on to explain what he meant by scientific art:

Perhaps the most prominent instance of the application of science to art . . . is the use of the elastic power of steam, applied to the operations of spinning and weaving and dressing fabrics for human wear. All this mighty discovery bears directly on the means of human subsistence and human comfort. . . . Hardly inferior in its importance is the application of the power of steam to transportation and conveyance by sea and by land. Who is so familiarized to the sight even now, as to look without wonder and amazement on the long train of cars, full of passengers and merchandise, drawn along our valleys, and the sides of our mountains themselves with a rapidity which holds competition [with] the winds?

This branch of the application of steam power is younger. It is not yet fully developed; but the older branch, its application to manufacturing machinery, is perhaps to be regarded as the more signal instance marking the great and glorious epoch of the application of science to the useful arts.

Webster concluded his celebration of the scientific arts with the claim that the "augmentation of wealth and comfort is general and diffusive, reaching to all classes, embracing all interests, and benefiting, not a part of society, but the whole."

The optimistic sense of progress implicit in Webster's speech was echoed again and again in the writings and rhetoric of the Jacksonian era. The majority of Americans felt that the future would be better than the past, just as democracy was better than monarchy, steam better than sail. Persons were never entirely satisfied with the present but were invariably expectant of a better future. "It is peculiarly the happy privilege of Americans," stated William James, a wealthy New York contractor and grandfather of the philosopher William James and the novelist Henry James, "to enjoy the blessings of hope and expectation."

As Webster's speech reflects, the expectations most commonly shared by Jacksonian Americans were unquestionably economic. "Go *ahead* is the real motto of the country," exclaimed a foreign visitor, "and every man does push on, to gain in advance of his neighbour." And another visitor noted:

The first thing which strikes a traveller in the United States is the innumerable multitude of those who seek to throw off their original condition. . . . No Americans are devoid of a yearning desire to rise. . . . It is not only a portion of the people which is busied with the amelioration of its social condition, but the whole community is engaged in the task.

The times favored risk and gambling, and almost everyone was out to accumulate riches. As the noted Unitarian clergyman William Ellery Channing observed: "How widely spread is the passion for acquisition, not for simple subsistence, but for wealth! What a rush into all departments of trade." Another contemporary wrote: "Americans boast of their skill in money making; and it is the only standard of dignity, and nobility, and worth . . . they endeavor to obtain it by every possible means."

Given the passion for wealth that dominated most Americans, it is not surprising to find that the era gave rise to the cult of the "self-made man"—a term coined by Senator Henry Clay in 1832. The idea of rising "from rags to riches" was common. President Jackson, having started as an orphan and being clearly self-made, was a fitting symbol for the age.

Examples of persons inspired to new aspirations by the rags-to-riches philosophy are many. Thomas Mellon, the founder of that family's fortune, recalled that as a young man of fourteen in 1828 he had been moved by the dream of economic betterment through reading the classic American success story, Benjamin Franklin's *Autobiography*.

> *I had not before imagined* [recalled Mellon] *any course in life superior to farming, but the reading of Franklin's life led me to question this view. For so poor and friendless a boy to be able to become a merchant or a professional man had before seemed an impossibility; but here was Franklin poorer than myself, who by industry, thrift and frugality had become learned and wise, and elevated to wealth and fame.*

Mellon soon left the family farm at Poverty Point and moved to nearby Pittsburgh where he quickly advanced as a lawyer, money lender, and finally banker.

That Mellon's quest for fortune led him from farm to city was not unusual for the age. Although agriculture remained the leading economic pursuit, ambitious Americans like Mellon were turning to more rapidly rewarding occupations in such fields as commerce and manufacturing. Wrote one young man at this time:

> *My disposition would not allow me to work on a farm. . . . I thought that I should be one of the happiest fellows in the world if I could only be rich, and I thought as others had begun with nothing and become men of fortune that I might. . . .*

One result of the rising economic expectations and consequent attractiveness of nonagrarian pursuits was the great urban growth of the era. Up to about 1820 the

The Wisconsin Emigrant

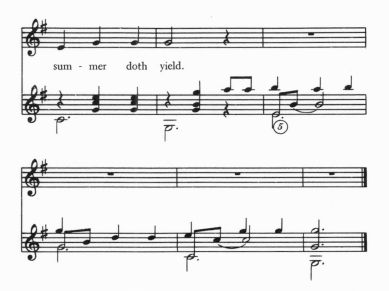

sum - mer   doth   yield.

"Oh husband, I've noticed with sorrowful heart,
You've neglected your oxen, your plough, and your cart.
Your sheep are disordered; at random they run,
And your new Sunday suit is now every day on.
Oh, stay on the farm and you'll suffer no loss,
For the stone that keeps rolling will gather no moss."

"Oh wife, let's go. Oh, don't let us wait.
Oh, I long to be there. Oh, I long to be great!
While you some rich lady—and who knows but I
Some governor may be before that I die?
While here I must labor each day in the field,
And the winter consumes all the summer doth yield."

"Oh husband, remember, that land is to clear,
Which will cost you the labor of many a year,
Where horses, sheep, cattle, and hogs are to buy—
And you'll scarcely get settled before you must die.
Oh, stay on your farm and you'll suffer no loss,
For the stone that keeps rolling will gather no moss."

"Oh wife, let's go. Oh, don't let us stay.
I will buy me a farm that is cleared by the way,
Where horses, sheep, cattle, and hogs are not dear,
And we'll feast on fat buffalo half of the year.
While here I must labor each day in the field,
And the winter consumes all the summer doth yield."

"Oh husband, remember, that land of delight,
Is surrounded by Indians who murder by night.
Your house they will plunder and burn to the ground,
While your wife and your children lie murdered around.
Oh, stay on the farm, and you'll suffer no loss,
For the stone that keeps rolling will gather no moss."

"Now wife, you've convinced me. I'll argue no more.
I never had thought of your dying before;
I love my dear children, although they are small—
But you, my dear wife, are more precious than all.
We'll stay on the farm, and suffer no loss,
For the stone that keeps rolling will gather no moss."

expansion of cities had been very slow at best. That decade, however, saw the beginning of the rapid urbanization of the nation which would so markedly differentiate modern America from its rural past. Writing in 1843, George Tucker, a professor at the University of Virginia, noted "that the increase of population in towns over 10,000 exceeded that of the whole population in the ratio of 50 to 32." This pleased Tucker since, as he claimed:

> The proportion between rural and town population of a country is an important fact in its interior economy and condition. It determines, in a great degree, its capacity for manufactures, the extent of its commerce, and the amount of its wealth. The growth of cities commonly marks the progress of intelligence and the arts, measures the sum of social enjoyment, and always implies increased mental activity.

Between 1820 and 1840 Philadelphia doubled in population from about 100,000 to well over 200,000. Pittsburgh during these same decades went from slightly over 7,000 to more than 21,000. New York, America's major metropolis, swelled from 123,000 to over 312,000 in these twenty years; while cities such as Chicago and Lowell, Massachusetts, which had not existed prior to 1820, were by 1840 major centers. In short, the rise of the modern city has been a fairly recent phenomenon beginning about the age of Jackson.

The cities of the Northeast became bustling commercial centers. Mrs. Anne Royall, a writer of travel books, described New York in the late 1820s:

> We landed in the city of New-York about 3 o'clock, and I took up my lodgings in Front street. . . . Next day,

South Street, New York City. Engraving by
William Bennett, 1828.

after breakfast, I bent my course toward the far famed Broadway; it is four miles long, and the side walks paved with flag [stone]. . . . It is impossible to give even an idea of the beauty and fashion displayed in Broadway on a fine day; the number of females, the richness and variety of dress, comprising all that can be conceived of wealth or skill, mocks description. . . . Next to Broadway, in point of beauty, is Hudson, Washington, Greenwich, and the Bowery; this last runs in a diagonal line, and joins Broadway. Pearl street, with many others first laid out, are narrow and crooked; there are, however, many handsome streets which cross at right angles, viz. Market, Grand, and Canal streets. Of all these streets, Pearl street does the most business, being the principal mart of the merchants. Wall street is also a place of much business, in it are the banking houses, exchange, brokers, insurance, auctioneers, and custom house offices; in short, all commercial business is transacted there. Nothing can exceed the throng of gentlemen in Wall street; particularly when their merchant ships arrive; on such occasions it is dangerous to walk in Wall street. . . . This street alone, may give a stranger an idea of the business and trade of New York. . . . But all this is only a drop in the bucket compared to that on the wharves . . . the warehouses, docks, shipyards, and auction stores, which occupy South, Front, and Water streets, pouring a flood of human beings. Here the sound of axes, saws, and hammers, from a thousand hands, there the ringing of the blacksmith's anvil; hard by the jolly tar with his heavo; the whole city surrounded with masts; the Hudson, East river, and the bay covered with vessels, some going out and some coming in, to say nothing of the steam-boats; in short, imag-

Fulton Street, New York City in the 1820's.

ine upwards of a hundred thousand people, all engaged in business; add to these some thousand strangers which swarm in the streets and public houses; such is New York.

In New England, Boston was the major metropolis. Here, too, newcomers noted an intensive interest in business. The English visitor Alexander Mackay wrote:

Along the wharves there is every appearance of great activity; and thickly strewn around you, are all the insignia of an extensive commerce. Raw cotton in countless bales; piles of manufactured goods for the South American and Chinese markets; whole acres covered with parallel rows of clean white barrels, some of them wellnigh bursting with flour, others full of salt; hogsheads of sugar, and others of leaking molasses; stacks of leather, and pyramids of marble blocks; bags of coffee, chests of tea, and bulging orange boxes, are discernible on every hand. By each pile is a clerk, busily noting all that may be added to, or subtracted from it; dealers, wholesale and retail, masters and men, consignors and consignees, and light and heavy porters, are bustling about. . . .

As might be expected, as you recede from the waterside, the business of the town assumes more of a retail character. . . . The shops are large, having in general, a wider frontage than with us. They are gorged with goods, so much so as literally to ooze out at doors and windows; and what a gaudy flaunting show they make! Piled in tempting masses on the hard brick pavement, you are ready to stumble over goods at every step you take, whilst from the upper windows stream whole pieces of flaring calicos and gaudy ribbons; the whole impressing one with the idea that business was making a holiday of it, and had donned, for the occasion, its most showy habiliments.

State Street, Boston during the 19th century.

Many of the goods displayed in the shop windows along New York's Broadway or Boston's Washington Street or Chestnut Street in Philadelphia were imported from various European countries and from as far away as China. But increasingly in the 1820s and 1830s articles of domestic manufacture were making their appearance —clocks and silverware from Connecticut; shoes and textiles from Massachusetts; furniture, leather, and iron goods from New York and Pennsylvania.

From the close of the War of 1812 to the 1850s the American economy was revolutionized with as far-reaching a set of consequences as our earlier political revolution. Turnpikes, canals, and, after 1828, railroads linked the vast and expanding country closer together, creating a national market for manufactures. A foreign visitor in the 1830s observed:

Town and country rival with each other in the eagerness of industrious pursuits. Machines are invented, new lines of communication established, and the depths of the sea explored to afford scope for the spirit of enterprise; and it is as if all America were but one gigantic workshop, over the entrance of which there is the blazing inscription "No admission here except on business."

Even automated mass production appeared at this time, as the description of a brass button factory by a British delegation of technical experts in the early 1850s illustrates:

The blanks [for buttons] being cut in thin brass, are put into a curved feeding-pipe, in which they descend to the level of the machine, by which a hole is stamped in

Acorn clock made in Bristol, Connecticut in the 1840's.

Office   Converting Furnaces

An industrial town in the early 19th century,
from a Currier and Ives lithograph.

the centre of each. Then the shank is formed by another
portion of the machine, from a continuous wire along
horizontally, the wire being shaped into the shank, and
pushed up into its proper place. These operations are
completed at the rate of 200 a minute, the only atten-
dance required being that of one person to feed this auto-
mation with the blanks and the wires.

Another traveler, a Scottish engineer named David
Stevenson, testified to the revolutionary progress of
American transportation as he witnessed it in 1837:

The zeal with which the Americans undertake, and
the rapidity with which they carry on every enterprise,
which has the enlargement of their trade for its object,
cannot fail to strike all who visit the United States as a
characteristic of the nation. . . . Thirty years ago [1807],

Gasometer   Rolling Mills N Currier's Lith. N.Y

it had but one steamer and one short canal, and now its
rivers and lakes are navigated by between five and six
hundred steamers, and its canals are upwards of two
thousand seven hundred miles in length; ten years ago,
there were but three miles of railway in the country, and
now there are no less than sixteen hundred miles in operation. These facts appear much more wonderful when
it is considered, that many of these great lines of communication are carried for miles in a trough, as it were,
cut through thick and almost impenetrable forests, where
it is no uncommon occurrence to travel for a whole day
without encountering a village or even a house.

Rapid urbanization, improved transportation, industrialization, many technological innovations, westward
expansion, rising economic aspirations, and greater
wealth were rapidly altering America. By the time Jack-

son assumed the presidency in 1829 the country appeared young, buoyant, and expanding. Optimism was widespread. The nation, intoned a Jacksonian Fourth of July orator, presents a "scene of unmingled prosperity and happiness. The ordinary citizen has his aspirations lifted up to the most exalted objects."

This optimistic belief that improvement of one's condition was possible made Americans a restless people. Haste was a national characteristic. As an American stated in 1836: "Rail Roads alone seem to be *understood*. Go ahead! is the order of the day. The whole continent presents a scene of scrabbling and roars with greedy hurry."

Francis Grund, an Austrian who had settled in America in the late 1820s, agreed.

The Americans seem to know no greater pleasure than that of going on fast, and accomplishing large distances in comparatively short times. . . . This continued motion of the Americans . . . resembles, on a huge scale, the vibrations of a pendulum. . . . This state of incessant excitement gives to the American an air of busy inquietude . . . which, in fact, constitutes their principle happiness.

However, despite the obvious optimism in the bustling Jacksonian era, not all persons were successful in their endeavors. In the pursuit of wealth, unfortunately, failures were as frequent as fortunes. For many Americans, the dreams of riches became nightmares of frustrated aspirations. Even reasonably successful individuals were goaded on by a mild discontent; few were satisfied with past accomplishments. In reflecting on this, a somewhat disaffected contemporary wrote that

Every one is tugging, trying, scheming to advance—to get ahead. It is a great scramble, in which all are troubled and none are satisfied. In Europe, the poor man, as a rule, knows that he must remain poor, and he submits to his lot, and tries to make the best of it. . . . Not so in America. Every other little ragged boy dreams of being President or millionaire. The dream may be a pleasant one while it lasts, but what of the disappointing reality? What of the excited, restless, feverish life spent in the pursuit of phantoms?

Alexis de Tocqueville's penetrating analysis of American society, *Democracy in America*, makes a similar point. "Democratic institutions," he wrote, "awaken and foster a passion for equality which they can never entirely satisfy." People felt that they had the opportunity of rising to the level of their fellow citizens, but were disappointed by their failure to reach any "level." Like a mule pursuing an outstretched carrot, Americans constantly sought an equality which, in Tocqueville's words,

perpetually retires from before them, yet without hiding itself from their sight, and in retiring draws them on. At every moment they think they are about to grasp it; it escapes from their hold. They are near enough to see its charms, but too far off to enjoy them, and before they have fully tasted its delights, they die. . . . In democratic ages enjoyments are more intense than in the ages of aristocracy, and especially the number of those who partake in them is larger: but, on the other hand, it must be *admitted that man's hopes and his desires are oftener blasted, the soul is more stricken and perturbed, and care itself more keen.*

While many persons were frustrated by apparent failure, others were upset by the speed of change itself. Prior to 1815 America had been a fairly stable society for nearly two centuries. Except for the Revolution, changes had occurred gradually and within accustomed institutional frameworks. After that date, however, new technology, new forms of economic organization, growing wealth, and geographical expansion presented a challenge to traditional values and ways. Everything appeared to be in flux. The novelist James Fenimore Cooper, who was rather anxious about the changes altering American society, had a character remark despairingly: "the whole country is in such a constant state of mutation, that I can only liken it to the game of children, in which, as one quits his corner another runs into it, and he that finds no corner to get into, is the laughing-stock of the others."

Surprisingly, one of the chief causes of consternation was the very material success of the American economy. The notion that morality thrived best on adversity was a common belief embedded in Protestant thought. Timothy Flint, a New England clergyman, on viewing the fashionable New York State resort at Saratoga Springs in the mid-1820s claimed that "here there is brought, full in your view, the great change, which the American character has recently undergone. A lover of the country cannot but regret to see that we are making such rapid strides in extravagance and luxury."

Flint's charge that fashionable living had undermined the virtues of hard work and had turned Americans toward a get-rich-quick scramble for money was echoed increasingly from the 1820s through the Civil War years. The Reverend Elihu Baldwin of New York, preaching in 1827, warned that "increasing wealth rolls the tide of fashionable vice over the land. Who that reflects, but must tremble for the consequences?" Similarly, the Reverend Caleb Stetson declared in 1842: "The inordinate pursuit of money for the gratification of avarice, vanity, pride, and ambition, has deeply corrupted the principles of the country, and nearly destroyed all generous public feeling."

Not only ministers, but laymen as well were disturbed by the seeming changes prosperity had wrought. According to a writer for the *American Review*, a journal of the Whig party, the restless pursuit of wealth made Americans a very unhappy people. The author explained this phenomenon in the following manner:

All strangers who come among us remark the excessive anxiety written in the American countenance. The widespread comfort, the facilities for livelihood, the spontaneous and cheap lands, the high price of labor are equally observed, and render it difficult to account for these lines of painful thoughtfulness. It is not poverty, nor tyranny, nor over-competition which produces this anxiety; that is clear. It is the concentration of the faculties upon an object, which in its very nature is unattainable —the perpetual improvement of the outward condition. There are no bounds among us to the restless desire to be better off; and this is the ambition of all classes of society. . . . No man in America is contented to be poor, or expects to continue so. There are here no established limits within which the hopes of any class of society must

Fashionable reception in New York, 1840.

be confined, as in other countries. There is consequently no condition of hopes realized, in other words, of contentment. . . .

America, this writer continued, is

in advance of the world in the great political principle, and we are now experiencing some of its first effects, let us not mistake these for the desirable fruits of freedom. Commerce is to become the universal pursuit of men. It is to be the first result of freedom, of popular institutions everywhere. . . . But while trade is destined to free and employ the masses, it is also destined to destroy for the time much of the beauty and happiness of every land. This has been the result in our own country. We are free. It is a glorious thing that we have no serfs, with the large and unfortunate exception of our slaves—no artificial distinctions—no acknowledged superiority of blood—no station which merit may not fill—no rungs in the social ladder to which the humblest may not aspire. But the excitement, the commercial activity, the restlessness, to which this state of things has given birth, is far from being a desirable restlessness or a natural condition. It is not natural to the human soul. It is good and hopeful to the interests of the race, but destructive to the happiness, and dangerous to the virtue of the generation exposed to it.

While numerous Americans appeared at times uneasy about the present and future, there was a common tendency to look back longingly to a supposed golden age. This was reflected in the nostalgic and sentimental tone of much popular culture. In reality Americans were aggressive and materialistic; but in popular fiction and poetry, characters were invariably portrayed as tender, moral, high-minded, and sentimental. Similarly in everyday life Americans were a highly mobile people busily engaged in settling the West and in building factories and cities; yet in literature the heroes and heroines were almost always homebodies, living contented nonmaterialistic lives in pastoral ancestral homesteads.

A good example of the sentimental, nostalgic, and antimaterialistic nature of American culture was the popular music of the period. In 1825 the 360-mile Erie Canal was completed linking the Hudson River with the Great Lakes and opening up an era of unprecedented materialism and expansionism. However, in a widely sung ballad commemorating this notable event, Samuel Woodworth, a popular poet, playwright, and journalist, specifically stressed the nonmonetary significance of the canal:

> Yet, it is not that Wealth now enriches the scene,
> Where the treasures of Art, and of Nature, convene;
> 'Tis not that this union [of waters] our coffers may fill—
> O! no—it is something more exquisite still.
>
> 'Tis, that Genius has triumph'd—and Science prevail'd,
> Tho' Prejudice flouted, and Envy assail'd,
> It is, that the vassals of Europe may see
> The progress of mind, in a land that is free.

The retrospective mood of the age combined with the reverence for family, nature, and place was captured in a popular song by George P. Morris, "Woodman, Spare that Tree" (1837):

> Woodman, spare that tree!
> Touch not a single bough;
> In youth it sheltered me,

And I'll protect it now;
'Twas my forefather's hand,
That placed it near his cot,
There woodman let it stand,
Thy axe shall harm it not!

There was then an ambivalence about Jacksonian America. On the one hand, it was a time of booming geographical and economic expansion which gave rise to great optimism about the future. Francis Grund captured this aspect of the national character when he wrote that:

the Americans love their country, not indeed, as it is; but as it will be. They do not love the land of their fathers; but they are sincerely attached to that which their children are destined to inherit. They live in the future, and make their country as they go on.

On the other hand, there exists ample evidence of far-ranging anxiety about the unknown future coupled with widespread nostalgia and regret for the forsaken past. Even the usually future-oriented politician Henry Clay could lament the fate of the restless American who in his wanderings became

separated, forever, from the roof under which the companions of his childhood were sheltered, from the trees which have shaded him from summer's heats, the spring from whose gushing fountain he has drunk in his youth, the tombs that hold the precious relics of his venerated ancestors.

The majority of Americans were ambivalent, being neither wholly optimistic and progressive nor wholly anxious and nostalgic. In most individuals the prevailing mood was one of hope and expectancy, though the doubts and the fears were never far from the surface. As today, this was an age of rapid and major economic, social, and political change, and (again like today) such change generated both new expectations and new insecurities. It is, in part, this ambivalence that makes the Jacksonian period so fascinating to study.

THE FACTORIES OF LOWELL
Industry Comes to America

*It was the Americans who first introduced the manufacture
of heavy goods by the application of the least amount of
labor to the greatest quantity of raw material, thus producing a description of goods cheaper to the consumer than
any heretofore existing. This system the English have been
obliged to follow.*

Nathan Appleton (1858)

If one wanted to show a foreign visitor a leading industrial city today, Detroit or Pittsburgh might well be
chosen. In pre-Civil War America, however, the model
American industrial community was unquestionably
Lowell, Massachusetts.

Lowell, an offspring of the industrial revolution, was
founded in 1822; but the genius responsible for its success was Francis Cabot Lowell who died in 1817 at the
age of forty-two. A member of a respected Boston mercantile family, Lowell had become interested in cotton
textile production while visiting England in 1811. The
favorable circumstances created for domestic manufacturers by the War of 1812 induced Lowell and several

other Boston merchants to establish a cotton factory. Although beginning with only a small mill in Waltham, Massachusetts, in 1813, the success of Lowell's ideas was almost immediately apparent. He perfected a power loom better than any then in use. Nathan Appleton, one of the original directors, wrote the following account of Francis Cabot Lowell's genius:

The power loom was at this time being introduced in England, but its construction was kept very secret, and after many failures, public opinion was not favorable to its success. Mr. Lowell had obtained all the information which was practicable about it, and was determined to perfect it himself. He was for some months experimenting at a store in Broad street, employing a man to turn a crank. It was not until the new building at Waltham was completed, and other machinery was running, that the first loom was ready for trial. Many little matters were to be overcome or adjusted, before it would work perfectly. Mr. Lowell said he did not wish me to see it until it was complete, of which he would give me notice. At length the time arrived. He invited me to go out with him and see the loom operate. I well recollect the state of admiration and satisfaction with which we sat by the hour, watching the beautiful movement of this new and wonderful machine, destined as it evidently was, to change the character of all textile industry. This was in the autumn of 1814.

Mr. Lowell was also responsible for a new type of industrial organization. Previous to the establishment of his Waltham factory, each textile mill did a particular operation. One would spin thread, another would weave

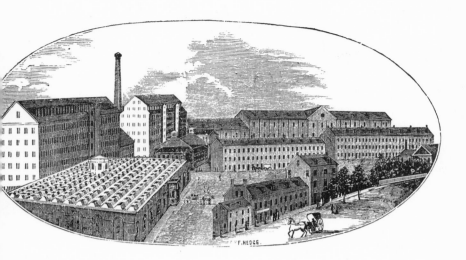

The Lowell Mills.

yarn, and so forth. "Mr. Lowell," again in Appleton's words,

adopted an entirely new arrangement, in order to save labor, in passing from one process to another . . . he is unquestionably entitled to the credit of being the first person who arranged all the processes for the conversion of cotton cloth, within the walls of the same building. It is remarkable how few changes have since been made from the arrangements established by him, in the first mill built at Waltham.

The Waltham factory continued to be successful after Lowell's death, and in the early 1820s the directors, known as the Boston Associates, decided to expand their operations. Land was purchased on the falls of the Merrimack River, located where that stream joined the Concord River, then a rural area of great beauty some twenty-five miles northwest of Boston. Here in 1822 construction was begun on a new industrial town, suitably named Lowell.

The directors were aware that many people believed industrial laborers to be "notoriously of the lowest character, for intelligence and morals." Appleton and the others seriously wondered "whether this degradation was the result of the peculiar occupation or of other and distinct causes."

They hoped at Lowell to prove that industrial employment did not inevitably result in physical and moral deterioration. It is clear from their journals and letters that these men conceived of their task as a distinctly moral one. They hoped to free this country from dependence on European manufactures and yet accomplish this without corrupting American society. "Ours is a great and novel experiment," proclaimed Appleton. "Whatever the result, it is our destiny to make it. It is our mission—our care should be to understand it and make it succeed."

Yet if these men were to establish an industrial Utopia, they realized that a new source of labor must be found. Where manufacturing had developed in the early nineteenth century, there appeared every indication that American factories would follow in the same exploitive path as European industries. The first factories of any significance in this country were the spinning mills of southern New England. These were small mills which turned raw cotton into yarn. The employers generally owned the town as well as the factory, and a type of neofeudalism developed. Whole families were hired; those with large numbers of children were preferred because the mills depended largely on child labor. Wages were low and frequently paid in the form of credits at the company's store. Poverty and exploitation were the rule, and few workingmen came out ahead financially.

While such a system had sufficed for these small spinning mills, clearly it was not a satisfactory model for the large-scale factories planned for Lowell by the Boston Associates. Therefore, rather than hiring whole families and relying heavily on child labor, the Boston industrialists hit upon the idea of employing unmarried New England farm women in their late teens and early twenties.

This plan had much to recommend it. As Appleton explained:

Cotton spinning.

There was little demand for female labor, as household manufacture was superseded by the improvements in machinery. Here was in New England a fund of labor, well educated and virtuous. It was not perceived how a profitable employment has any tendency to deteriorate the character. The most efficient guards were adopted in establishing boarding houses, at the cost of the Company, under the charge of respectable women with every provision for religious worship. Under these circumstances, the daughters of respectable farmers were readily induced to come into these mills for a temporary period.

This system proved to be highly successful. Lowell's heavily mechanized and financed factories easily withstood British competition and soon were returning dividends that averaged close to 20 percent annually and in some years as much as 40 percent. Success led to further expansion, and within a generation the Boston Associates had major mills in operation throughout southern Maine and New Hampshire and northern Massachusetts. Operations at Lowell itself were also expanded. In 1831 a contemporary noted that this town employed

nearly 6000 persons in cotton manufactures alone, and produced more than two thirds of a million of yards [of cloth] per week, or about thirty-six millions of yards per annum. . . . The whole may be estimated at 10 cents per yard; making 3,600,000 dollars . . . per annum.

But the greatest triumph of the Boston investors was in creating a progressive industrial image acceptable to agrarian America. In this regard Lowell was their show place.

Only four years after Lowell's inception a noted

British traveler, Captain Basil Hall, made a point of visiting these mills. Struck by the vivid contrast between Lowell and English factory towns, Hall in his popular *Travels in North America* portrayed this New World manufactory in glowing terms:

The whole discipline, ventilation, and other arrangements appeared to be excellent, of which the best proof was the healthy and cheerful look of the girls, all of whom, by the way, were trigged out with much neatness and simplicity, and wore high tortoise-shell combs at the back of their heads.

Awakened at six in the morning by the tolling of the factory bells, Hall,

on looking from the window, saw the whole space between the factories and the village speckled over with girls, nicely dressed, and glittering with bright shawls and showy-colored gowns and gay bonnets, all streaming along to their business, with an air of lightness, and elasticity of step, implying an obvious desire to get to their work.

Between Hall's 1827 visit and the Civil War, virtually all of the many foreign travelers in America went to admire Lowell. It became a standard stop on a traveler's itinerary, as were Niagara Falls, Washington, a slave auction, a prison, a revival meeting, and an Indian encampment. With but few exceptions, Lowell was described as "clean," "fresh," "new," "moral," "healthy." To the Frenchman Michel Chevalier, a student of industrialism, Lowell in 1834 was "neat, orderly, quiet, and prudent," unlike any industrial center he had ever seen.

Harriet Martineau, a curious, sympathetic, ear-trumpeted English tourist, visiting Lowell that same year, noted approvingly the "neat, spacious" town with its churches, lecture hall, library, and "well-dressed young ladies."

When Charles Dickens, the great English novelist, came to Lowell in 1842, the town was nearly two decades old; yet it was the quality of newness that most impressed him:

The very river that moves the machinery in the mills . . . seems to acquire a new character from the fresh buildings of bright red brick and painted wood among which it takes its course; and to be as light-headed, thoughtless, and brisk a young river, in its murmurings and tumblings, as one would desire to see. One would swear that every "Bakery," "Grocery," and other kind of store, took its shutters down for the first time, and started in business yesterday.

Native-born American dignitaries also stopped frequently at Lowell and admired its female employees. "Very pretty women, by the Eternal!" proclaimed President Jackson on his 1833 visit. A year later Colonel Davy Crockett, the famed frontiersman, was also impressed:

We stopped at a large stone house at the head of the falls of the Merrimack River, and . . . went down among the factories. The dinner-bells were ringing and the folks pouring out of the houses like bees out of gum. I looked at them as they passed, all were well-dressed, lively and genteel in their appearance, indeed the girls looked as if they were coming from a quilting frolic. . . . I went among the young girls, and talked with many of them. Not one expressed herself as tired of her employment, or

Lucy Larcom.

oppressed with work; all talked well, and looked healthy. Some of them were very handsome.

The view of Lowell held by the female workers themselves seldom corresponded with the pleasant picture painted by visitors. Their actual working conditions, which were far from idyllic, will be treated in the following chapter. Nevertheless, at least some of them did have a sense of participating in a novel experiment that presaged great things for America's future. One such individual was Lucy Larcom. Miss Larcom had been brought to Lowell as a small child when her widowed mother had taken a job there as a keeper of one of the company boardinghouses.

The income from the boardinghouse proved insufficient, and one day Lucy overheard her mother say "in a distressed tone, 'The children will have to leave school and go into the mill.'" Before her twelfth birthday Lucy was sent to work in one of the Lowell factories. Looking back on this experience in later life, she recalled going to her "first day's work in the mill with a light heart."

The novelty of it made it seem easy, and it really was not hard, just to change the bobbins on the spinning-frames every three quarters of an hour or so, with half a dozen other little girls who were doing the same thing.

For a little while it was only a new amusement; I liked it better than going to school and "making believe" I was learning when I was not. And there was a great deal of play mixed with it. We were not occupied more than half the time. The intervals were spent frolicking around among the spinning-frames, teasing and talking to

A Paper of Pins

you ____ will mar - ry me. ____

I won't accept your paper of pins,
If that's the way our love begins,
And I'll not marry, marry you,
And I'll not marry you.

I'll give to you a dress of red,
Stitched all around with golden thread,
If you will marry, marry me,
If you will marry me.

I won't accept your dress of red,
Stitched all around with golden thread,
And I'll not marry, marry you,
And I'll not marry you.

I'll give to you a dress of green,
That you may be as any queen,
If you will marry, marry me,
If you will marry me.

I'll not accept your dress of green,
That I may be as any queen,
And I'll not marry, marry you,
And I'll not marry you.

I'll give to you a blue silk gown,
With yellow tassels hanging down,
If you will marry, marry me,
If you will marry me.

I'll not accept your blue silk gown,
With yellow tassels hanging down,
And I'll not marry, marry you,
And I'll not marry you.

I'll give to you a coach and four,
That you may visit from door to door,
If you will marry, marry me,
If you will marry me.

I'll not accept your coach and four,
That I may visit from door to door,
And I'll not marry, marry you,
And I'll not marry you.

I'll give to you the keys to my chest,
That you may have money at your request,
If you will marry, marry me,
If you will marry me.

I will accept the keys to your chest,
That I may have money at my request,
And I will marry, marry you,
And I will marry you!

Now I see, as plain as can be,
You love my money, and you don't love me,
And I'll not marry, marry you,
And I'll not marry you.

the older girls, or entertaining ourselves with games and stories in a corner, or exploring, with the overseer's permission, the mysteries of the carding-room, the dressing-room, and the weaving-room.

The novelty soon wore off, however.

I never cared much for machinery [she remembered]. *The buzzing and hissing and whizzing of pulleys and rollers and spindles and flyers around me often grew tiresome. . . . It was not, and could not be, the right sort of life for a child.*

If only she could go to school, Lucy felt she would find fulfillment.

But alas! I could not go. The little money I could earn—one dollar a week, besides the price of my board— was needed in the family, and I must return to the mill. It was a severe disappointment to me, though I did not say so at home.

Amid the whirring spindles and rolling waterwheels, Lucy dreamed of a better life.

I did need and want . . . to study. I think the resolution was then formed, inwardly, that I would go to school again, some time, whatever happened. I went back to my work, but now without enthusiasm. I had looked through an open door that I was not willing to see shut upon me.

I began to reflect upon life rather seriously for a girl of twelve or thirteen. What was I here for? What could I make of myself? . . . It was seldom said to little girls, as it always has been said to boys, that they ought to have some definite plan, while they were children, what to be and do when they were grown up. There was usually but one path open to them, to become good wives and housekeepers. . . . But girls, as well as boys, must often have been conscious of their own peculiar capabilities—must have desired to cultivate and make use of their individual powers. . . . When I thought what I should best like to do, my first dream . . . about it was that it would be a fine thing to be a school-teacher. . . . Afterward, when I heard that there were artists, I wished I could some time be one.

But during the long hours of factory work, Lucy's most persistent dream was to become an author. As she worked, verses "seemed to fly into my mind."

I knew I should write; I could not help doing that, for my hand seemed instinctively to move towards pen and paper in moments of leisure. But to write anything worth while, I must have mental cultivation; so, in preparing myself to teach, I could also be preparing myself to write.

This was the plan that indefinitely shaped itself in my mind as I returned to my work in the spinning-room.

Lucy Larcom's dream did become a reality. She obtained an education and in later life won fame as a poet. She also discovered in the mills that many others of the young women had higher aspirations than a lifetime of factory work.

None of us [she wrote] had the least idea of continuing at that kind of work permanently. Our composite photograph, had it been taken, would have been the representative New England girlhood of those days. We had all been fairly educated at public or private schools, and many of us were resolutely bent upon obtaining a better education. Very few among us were without some distinct plan for bettering the condition of themselves and those they loved. . . . For twenty years or so, Lowell might have been looked upon as a rather select industrial school for young people.

Another aspect of early Lowell that impressed Miss Larcom was its rural appearance:

Nature came very close to the millgates. . . . There was green grass all around them; violets and wild geraniums grew by the canals; and long stretches of open land between the corporation buildings and the streets made the town seem country-like.

In part the rural look of Lowell and other early factory towns resulted from the fact that waterpower rather than steam was utilized. As a New Hampshire mill owner wrote in the early 1830s:

In this country water-power is almost exclusively used in manufactures, and, on account of its greater cheapness, the day must be far distant indeed, when steam power will be extensively used; the consequence is, that the manufacturing population must be scattered. We have no Manchesters on this side of the Atlantic, while our thousand rivers and streams afford an inexhaustible supply of unimproved power.

But this ruralness also stemmed from a conscious effort on the part of manufacturers to avoid the evils of European industrialism. To many Americans the degradation of the Old World industrial worker was more the result of urban conditions than of industry itself.

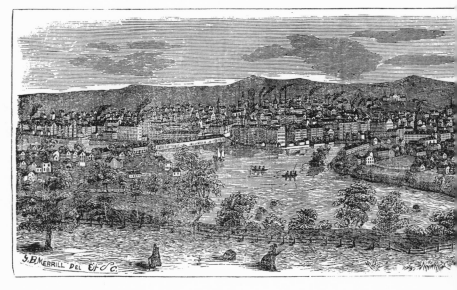

View of Lowell.

Patrick Tracy Jackson, one of Lowell's originators, reporting for a group of northern manufacturers in 1832, stated:

In Europe, manufactures are established in large cities, the business is followed from parent to child, and wages are so miserably low, that few families can be supported without . . . aid. One consequence of this abject poverty is that children are set to work at a very tender age, and have no time allowed for education, literary or moral. In the United States, manufactories are dispersed through the country.

The rural character of Lowell and other early factory towns allowed persons to hold to the Jeffersonian concepts of the moral virtues of country life while simultaneously participating in industrialization. The advocates of manufacturing not only argued that such employment was moral, but they also claimed that increased industrialization would stimulate farmers to become more moral and productive themselves. A representative proponent of this position was George S. White, the first biographer of Samuel Slater, who founded America's earliest mechanized textile factory. Writing in the mid-1830s, White stated:

A nation peopled only by farmers must be a region of indolence and misery. If the soil is naturally fertile, little labour will produce abundance; but for want of exercise even that little labour will be burdensome and often neglected. Want will be felt in the midst of abundance. . . . Those therefore who wish to make agriculture flourish in any country, can have no hope of succeeding in the attempt but by bringing commerce and manu-

factures to her aid; which by taking from the farmer his superfluous produce, gives spirit to his operations, and life and activity to his mind.

Such arguments, together with rising prosperity, won for the New England textile manufacturers and other industrialists a large measure of public support and worldwide fame. Industrial production grew rapidly. By 1835 an observant American noted that "manufacturing, instead of going on quietly and single-handed in private families, with immense labour, grows into large establishments, which employ and bring into association, masses of the population."

Two years later, Francis Grund clearly perceived the enthusiasm with which Americans accepted industrialization:

The manufactures of the United States have kept equal pace with the extension of commerce. The states of Massachusetts, Pennsylvania, New York, and New Jersey have taken the lead; but the same spirit of enterprise is manifesting itself in every quarter of the union. America possesses all the requisites of a manufacturing country, water, coal, and a highly ingenious, inventive population. . . . There is scarcely an article which does not furnish them with new means of exercising their ingenuity. Thus a large trade is carried on, by the people of New England, in painted chairs, which are sent by the thousands all over the United States, and also exported to South America, and the West Indies. The shoe trade of some of the towns in the neighborhood of Boston is hardly less remarkable, the value of nearly two millions of dollars having been manufactured last

A New England mill around 1850.

year and sent to the west alone. The state of Connecticut possesses the most extensive wooden clock manufactories in the world; affording them at about half the price of those made in the Black Forest.

Yet, despite such praise for manufactures, not all Americans greeted the industrialization of their country with unbounded enthusiasm. For workers, as shall be seen in the next chapter, the negative effects of factory labor often outweighed its benefits.

■3■

THE TARTARUS
OF MAIDS AND MECHANICS

*We do not believe there can be a single person found . . .
who ever thanked God for permission to work in a cotton
mill.*

Seth Luther (1833)

At the time when many American and foreign dignitaries were singing the praises of Lowell and New England industry generally, the young novelist Herman Melville saw things differently. In the early 1850s he published a short story entitled "The Tartarus of Maids."* Though set in a paper mill, the tale clearly attacked the farm-women labor system made famous at Lowell. The story opens with a man traveling toward the paper mill across the "bright farms and sunny meadows" of New England. But his route becomes more desolate as he nears the mill. He passes "among bleak hills," between the "cloven walls of haggard rock," through a gorge at "Black Notch" and into a hollow known as "the Devil's Dungeon" cut by the "Blood River."

* "Tartarus" in Greek mythology was a sunless abyss below Hades where Zeus imprisoned the Titans.

Arriving finally at the mill in weather that has turned biting cold, the man enters. Inside his first view is of "rows of blank-looking counters" behind which "sat rows of blank-looking girls, with blank, white folders in their blank hands, all blankly folding blank paper." The air inside the mill is hot and "swam with . . . fine, poisonous particles, which from all sides darted . . . into the lungs." The only sound that the man hears is

the low, steady over-ruling hum of the iron animals. The human voice was banished from the spot. Machinery— that vaunted slave of humanity—here stood menially served by human beings, who served mutely and cringingly as the slave serves the Sultan. The girls did not so much seem accessory wheels to the general machinery as mere cogs to the wheels.

Dominating Melville's fictitious factory is "the great machine" that makes the paper. Gazing "upon this inflexible iron animal," the visitor is awestruck:

Always, more or less, machinery of this ponderous, elaborate sort strikes, in some moods, strange dread into the human heart, as some living, panting Behemoth might. But what made the thing I saw so specially terrible to me was the metallic necessity, the unbudging fatality which governed it. . . . I seemed to see, glued to the pallid incipience of the pulp, the yet more pallid faces of all the pallid girls I had eyed that day. Slowly, mournfully, beseechingly, yet unresistingly, they gleaned along, their agony dimly outlined on the imperfect paper.

Having inspected the factory, the stranger inquires why it is that the workers, regardless of age, "are indiscriminately called girls, never women?" He is told that it is because they are unmarried:

For our factory here, we will not have married women; they are apt to be off-and-on too much. We want none but steady workers: twelve hours to the day, day after day, through the three hundred and sixty-five days, excepting Sundays, Thanksgiving, and Fast-days.

With a silent bow to the "pale virginity" of the maids, the traveler rides away from the artificial world of the "iron animals" back to "inscrutable nature," exclaiming as he leaves the Devil's Dungeon, "Oh! Tartarus of Maids!"

Though Melville's fictitious factory was in some ways farfetched, it came closer to capturing the realities of New England industrial labor than the idealized picture frequently painted by visiting travelers. Several evils of industrialization stand out in Melville's story. First, the workers were treated by their employers as mere commodities, not as people. Second, the machinery with its methodical regularity was dehumanizing and put great pressure on the employees. Third, the working conditions—characterized by noise, heat, bad air, and long hours—were unhealthy. Finally, the factory was far removed from the beauties of nature and, in fact, was an *unnatural* intrusion upon such beauties. These evils, though somewhat exaggerated by Melville, all could be seen at Lowell and other factories of the 1840s.

Melville was not alone in criticizing the working conditions to which the female employees of Lowell were subject. In 1840, more than a dozen years prior to the publication of Melville's "Tartarus of Maids," Orestes

Orestes Augustus Brownson, engraving by A. L. Dick, 1843.

A. Brownson, a radical New Englander, published two widely circulated essays on "The Laboring Classes" which sharply attacked the Lowell system. Taking a broad view of the industrial revolution, Brownson claimed that

No one can observe the signs of the times with much care without perceiving that a crisis as to the relation of wealth and labor is approaching. It is useless to shut our eyes to the fact, and like the ostrich fancy ourselves secure because we have so concealed our heads that we see not the danger. We or our children will have to meet this crisis. The old war between the King and the Barons is well nigh ended, and so is that between the Barons and the Merchants and Manufacturers, landed capital and commercial capital. The businessman has become the peer of my Lord. And now commences the new struggle between the operative and his employer, between wealth and labor.

Writing specifically of the contrast between the realities of Lowell labor and the rosy views of visitors, Brownson claimed:

We pass through our manufacturing villages; most of them appear neat and flourishing. The operatives are well dressed and, we are told, well paid. They are said to be healthy, contented, and happy. This is the fair side of the picture; the side exhibited to distinguished visitors. There is a dark side, moral as well as physical. Of the common operatives, few, if any, by their wages, acquire a competence. . . . The great mass wear out their health, spirits, and morals without becoming one whit better off than when they commenced labor. The bills

Mill workers in the mid-19th century.

of mortality in these factory villages are not striking, we admit, for the poor girls when they can toil no longer go home to die. The average life—working life, we mean —of the girls that come to Lowell . . . is only about three years. What becomes of them? Few of them ever marry; fewer still ever return to their native places with reputations unimpaired. "She has worked in a factory," is almost enough to damn to infamy the most worthy and virtuous girl. We know no sadder sight on earth than one of our factory villages presents when the bell, at break of day . . . calls out its hundreds or thousands of operatives. We stand and look at these hard-working men and women hurrying in all directions and ask ourselves where go the proceeds of their labors? The man who employs them and for whom they are toiling as so many slaves is one of our city nabobs, reveling in luxury; or he is a member of our legislature, enacting laws to put money in his own pocket; or he is a member of Congress, contending for a high tariff to tax the poor for the benefit of the rich; or in these times [a period of depression] he is shedding crocodile tears over the deplorable condition of the poor laborer, while he docks his wages twenty-five per cent.

So bad did Brownson find factory labor that he compared it unfavorably with slavery:

Wages is a cunning device of the devil for the benefit of tender consciences who would retain all the advantages of the slave system without the expense, trouble, and odium of being slaveholders.

Brownson's statements, like Melville's, were somewhat exaggerated, particularly in his references to the loss of moral virtue by the operatives. But his analysis does show a keen understanding of the detrimental effects the machine and the corporation were having on the economic relationships between classes. Like Karl Marx, who was soon to express similar theories in his powerful *Communist Manifesto* (1848), Brownson saw that a person operating a machine owned by another was in an inherently unequal position.

Melville and Brownson were witnesses to the demise of Lowell as an industrial idyll. Yet, by present-day standards, even in its earliest years Lowell would not be considered an admirable model for a factory town. The oft-praised paternalism of Lowell was double edged and aimed primarily at creating a docile and disciplined labor force. The women on taking jobs had to sign contracts stipulating among other things that:

All persons employed by the company must devote themselves assiduously to their duty during working hours. They must be capable of doing the work which they undertake, or use all their efforts to this effect. They must on all occasions, both in their words and in their actions, show that they are penetrated by a laudable love of temperance and virtue, and animated by a sense of their moral and social obligations.

Other rules specified fines for being even a minute late for work, forbade anyone from leaving the factory during working hours without the overseer's permission, and called for at least a year's employment with two weeks' notice of intent to leave. In addition to such elaborate regulations, factory managers made strong efforts to prevent employees from organizing to protest their grievances. Workers known to be agitators were fired and blacklisted from obtaining employment in other mills.

Working hours were extremely long, averaging over seventy-five hours per week at weekly wages ranging from one dollar to two dollars (exclusive of room and board).

The atmosphere within the mills where the long hours of labor were spent was unpleasant. As one observer noted on entering a Lowell factory in the mid-1830s:

The din and clatter of these five hundred looms, under full operation, struck us on first entering as something frightful and infernal, for it seemed such an atrocious violation of one of the faculties of the human soul, the sense of hearing. . . . The atmosphere of such a room . . . is charged with cotton filaments and dust. . . . Although the day was warm, we remarked that the windows were down. We asked the reason, and a young woman answered very naïvely, and without seeming to be in the least aware that this privation of fresh air was anything else than perfectly natural, that "when the wind blew, the threads did not work well."

Even in the boardinghouses, this same source continued, there was little peace since "the young women sleep upon an average six in a room, three beds to a room. There is no privacy, no retirement, here."

If conditions were this bad in the mills, one might wonder why women were attracted to Lowell at all. One explanation was the lack of other moneymaking alternatives. Employment of women outside the home traditionally had been limited to domestic service and

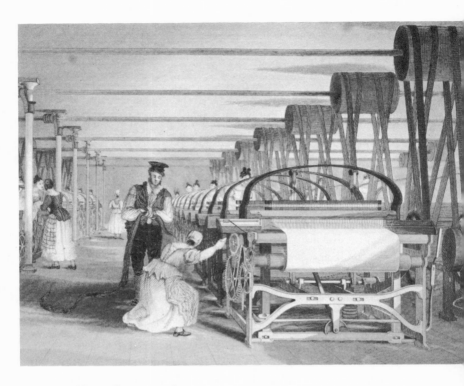

Power loom weaving.

schoolteaching. Neither of these occupations paid well, and the former was considered socially degrading. Mill work, therefore, however toilsome, offered women an opportunity to save some money and gain a certain sense of independence. As one of the Lowell workers wrote, the work was preferable "to going out as 'hired help.' " To persons who had seldom had money of their own, the Lowell wages could seem substantial, and since most farm women were accustomed to laboring from dawn to dusk on the farm, the Lowell hours did not at first appear excessive. There was the excitement of being away from home, meeting new people, and broadening one's social and intellectual horizons.

Some women came to work at Lowell because of the glowing reports about it; most of these persons, however, were quickly disillusioned. For, as one of the mill workers recalled, "instead of Arcadia, they found a place of matter-of-fact toil."

While Lowell's paternalism was not altogether beneficial to workers in the beginning, it became less so as years went on. The financial success of the Boston Associates led them to expand and encouraged others to establish competing textile mills. In turn this competition caused the price of cotton cloth to drop. In order to maintain high dividends, therefore, the Lowell owners pressured their hired factory managers to speed up production and reduce labor costs. As early as 1830 both the hours of labor and the number of machines tended by each operative were increased. In 1834 and again in 1836 wages were cut from 15 percent to 25 percent. Piece rates were introduced as a method of making women work harder, and premiums were granted to overseers who were able to increase production.

By the 1840s workers were tending four looms, yet earning no more than persons who had tended one or two looms a decade earlier. Just how far Lowell had fallen from its image as an industrial Utopia was indicated in a candid statement by one of the mill managers in the mid-1840s: "I regard my work-people just as I regard my machinery. So long as they can do my work for what I choose to pay them, I keep them, getting out of them all I can."

The women did not accept the increasingly harsh dictates of the impersonal corporation without protest. Despite management opposition, workers did organize. Following a pay reduction in 1834, the first strike occurred. The disapproving reporter of the *Boston Transcript* described it as follows:

We learn that extraordinary excitement was occasioned at Lowell, last week, by an announcement that the wages paid in some of the departments would be reduced 15 percent on the 1st of March. The reduction principally affected the female operatives, and they held several meetings . . . at which a young woman presided, who took an active part in persuading her associates to give notice that they should quit the mills. . . .

On Friday morning, the woman referred to was dismissed, by the Agent . . . and on leaving the office . . . waved her calash [bonnet] in the air, as a signal to the others, who were watching from the windows, when they immediately "struck" and assembled about her, in despite of the overseers.

The number soon increased to nearly 800. A procession was formed, and they marched about the town, to the amusement of a mob of idlers and boys, and, we are

Lowell Offering (*Lowell workers' magazine*),
1845.

sorry to add, not altogether to the credit of Yankee girls.
. . . We are told that one of the leaders mounted a
stump and made a flaming . . . speech on the rights of
women and the iniquities of the "monied aristocracy,"
which produced a powerful effect on her auditors, and
they determined to "have their way if they died for it."

The women did not have their way in this strike or
in others that followed. But they were determined. New
wage cuts in 1836 led to another strike. The weavers
were the first to walk out. Other sections of the mill
soon followed. An eleven-year-old girl, Harriet Hanson,
was working in the spinning room at the time. She re-
membered the older workers discussing the strike but
being undecided about joining. Harriet heard them

asking each other, "Would you?" or "Shall we turn
out?" and not one of them having the courage to lead
off, I, began to think they would not go out, after all
their talk, became impatient and started on ahead, saying
with childish bravado, "I don't care what you do, I am
going to turn out, whether any one else does or not"; and
I marched out and was followed by the others.

The striking women, some fifteen hundred strong,
marched through the streets of Lowell singing a parody
of an old song, "I Won't be a Nun":

> Oh, isn't it a pity, such a pretty girl as I
> Should be sent to the factory to pine away and die?
> Oh! I will not be a slave
> For I'm so fond of liberty
> That I cannot be a slave.

But the more they attempted to win better conditions,

the more determined the managers were to suppress their organized efforts. Working conditions continued to deteriorate. By the 1840s many of New England's female workers were leaving, driven from the factories by the long hours, low wages, rigid discipline, and speeded-up labor. Those who remained were becoming a more permanent factory population dependent on industrial employment for a meager subsistence.

As the more ambitious women left Lowell, the famed labor system rapidly broke down. At first the management tried to perpetuate it, sending out agents into northern Maine, Vermont, and New Hampshire to bring in new farm women. A reporter, sympathetic to the working women, commented on this operation in the mid-1840s as follows:

Observing a singular-looking "long, low, black" wagon passing along the street, we made inquiries respecting it, and were informed that it was what we term a "slaver." She makes regular trips to the north . . . cruising around in Vermont and New Hampshire, with a "commander" whose heart must be as black as his craft, who is paid a dollar a head for all he brings to the market [mills], and more in proportion to the distance—if they bring them such a distance that they cannot easily get back.

This is done by "hoisting false colors," and representing to the girls that they can tend more machinery than is possible, and that the work is so very neat, and the wages such that they can dress in silks and spend half their time in reading.

But even the use of "slavers" failed to bring in sufficient laborers. From the mid-1840s on, this practice was increasingly abandoned in favor of hiring the recently arrived immigrants streaming in from Ireland, Germany, and French Canada. The end result was that Lowell, which had been the New World exemplar of industrial Utopia, became instead just one of many competing mill towns, successful because of ruthless exploitation of an increasingly permanent and stratified labor force.

If the story of Lowell were exceptional, its deterioration would be of little note in the history of Jacksonian America. But Lowell was not the exception. The revolutions in industry and transportation which set the era off from previous periods created a growing class of wage workers who in most instances labored long hours for low wages in ill-ventilated and poorly lighted mills, living in crowded, filthy housing. In fact, the only unusual thing about Lowell was its distinctly unproletarian appearance in the early years. Most other factory towns, in New England and elsewhere, seem almost to have been conceived in squalor, never experiencing a utopian phase.

In Pennsylvania, for instance, cities such as Philadelphia and Pittsburgh became crowded, dirty industrial centers. A Pittsburgh physician testifying before a Pennsylvania Senate committee investigating industrial conditions in 1837, related that

factory children generally . . . live in confined, narrow, ill-ventilated rooms and cellars, among the poorest of the poor, in old frame houses where the atmosphere is peculiarly bad, highly impregnated with putrid miasmata [germs], arising from the offals and miserable population —each family having, in many instances, only a single room for all purposes of life.

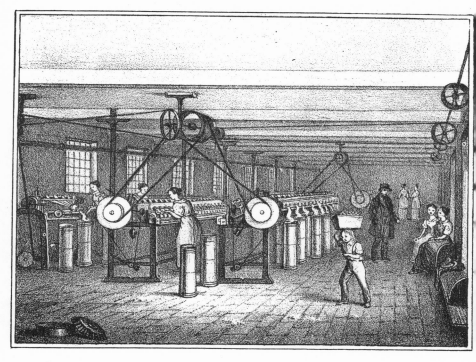

Bobbin and drawing frames in a cotton mill.

The same 1837 Senate committee hearing also revealed that children under the age of twelve made up about one-fifth of the work force in Pennsylvania's textile factories. Their wages ranged from as low as 12½ cents a week to 75 cents. Women workers, who also made up a sizable portion of the textile labor force, received slightly higher pay, anywhere from 50 cents to $2.60 per week. The presence of large numbers of women and children in these mills made it difficult on occasions for men to find employment.

In general, Pennsylvania workers felt a sense of degradation and a loss of status and independence. As a Philadelphia worker complained in 1827: "Those [laborers] who are toiling day after day, spending their strength, and wasting their health in the production of wealth are doomed not only to poverty with all its attendant inconvenience, but even to contempt."

Laborers in New York, the nation's wealthiest and most populous state, experienced a similar sense of loss confronting the changes wrought by industrialization. An 1829 writer for the prolabor *New York Evening Journal* bemoaned that "although the Mechanics are the most useful and powerful body of men in the community . . . they are . . . considered in many points inferior. . . . Is it a stain upon the character to gain an honest livelihood by useful industry?"

New York City was a major industrial center by the Jacksonian period. Of its many industries the most exploitive was the ready-made clothing business. Numerous sweatshops thrived on the labor of women needle-workers. A reformer of the early 1830s estimated that a seamstress working a full week could on the average sew nine shirts. Prices paid for this work varied from 6 cents to 9 cents per shirt, giving these women a weekly wage of 54 cents to 90 cents "for the incessant application of a human body, during thirteen or fourteen hours a day, for the payment of rent, the purchase of food, clothes, drink, soap, candles and fuel."

In 1833 a New York doctor attributed the evident increase in prostitution to the poor pay in the needle trades:

My profession affords me many and unpleasant opportunities of knowing the wants of those unfortunate females, who try to earn an honest subsistence by the needle, and to witness the struggles often made by honest pride and destitution. I could cite many instances of young and even middle-aged women, who have been "lost to virtue," apparently by no other cause than the lowness of wages, and THE ABSOLUTE IMPOSSIBILITY OF PROCURING THE NECESSARIES OF LIFE BY HONEST INDUSTRY.

Those employed in factories or sweatshops were not the only oppressed workers in the Jacksonian period. There also existed large numbers of unskilled common laborers hired for such things as construction work on canals, turnpikes, and railroads. Such work was hard, low paying, unhealthy, socially degrading, and seasonal. Many Irish and German immigrants took such employment because little else was available to them. Mathew Carey, a middle-class humanitarian, gave the following description of canal work in 1833:

Thousands of our labouring people travel hundreds of miles in quest of employment on canals, at 62, 75, and

Across the Western Ocean

Oh, the times are hard and the wag-es are low, A-mel - ia, where you___ bound for? The Rock - y Moun - tains is my home, A-

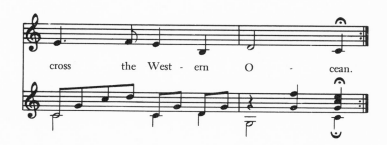

cross   the West - ern   O - cean.

Beware these packet ships I say,
    Amelia, where you bound for?
They'll steal your stores and clothes away,
    Across the Western Ocean.

There's Liverpool Pat with his tarpaulin hat,
    Amelia, where you bound for?
And Yankee John the packet rat,
    Across the Western Ocean.

Father and Mother, say good bye,
    Amelia, where you bound for?
Brother and sister, don't you cry,
    Across the Western Ocean.

87 cents per day, paying a dollar and a half or two dollars a week for their board, leaving families behind, depending on them for support. They labour frequently in marshy grounds which destroys their health, often irrevocably. They return to their poor families—with ruined constitutions, with a sorry pittance, most laboriously earned, and take to their beds sick and unable to work. Hundreds are swept off annually, many of them leaving numerous and helpless families. Notwithstanding their wretched fate, their places are quickly supplied by others, although death stares them in the face.

While the worst working conditions in the 1820s and 1830s were experienced by common laborers and factory operatives, those most vocal about deteriorating conditions were skilled craftsmen. From the colonial period through the early nineteenth century, trained artisans working as shoemakers, tailors, cabinet makers, printers, or at other skills had enjoyed esteemed positions in American society. Most such workers had learned their trades as young men while apprenticed to master craftsmen. Apprentices after a number of years moved up in rank, becoming journeymen. Journeymen in turn worked to become master craftsmen and owners of their own shops. Such a system did not divide employees from employers. The master and his journeymen and apprentices shared the labor and the profits, generally working together in a small shop producing goods ordered for the local market.

By the mid-1820s this harmonious system was breaking down. The revolutions in industry and transportation gradually made the small craft shop obsolete. In order to survive, master craftsmen were forced to produce more goods at a cheaper price. Pressured in this way, the master tried to maintain his profits by reducing the wages paid to his journeymen and apprentices.

To journeymen accustomed to a respected and reasonably remunerated job with the prospect of future advancement, the collapse of the traditional system came as a shock. They became insecure concerning their status and aware for the first time that their interests, in the words of the New York journeymen printers, "are *separate* and in some respects *opposite* to those of the employers." The sense of outrage was evidenced in much of the labor writing and rhetoric of the Jacksonian era. "Monopolists and capitalists," claimed an 1830 labor newspaper, have usurped the rights of journeymen, "abridging their privileges by opposing them in their business with the advantage of a large capital." This article continued:

Men who are not mechanics [not trained in the apprenticeship system] *are engaged in mechanical concerns . . . at the expense of the interest of the legitimate mechanics; and in many cases, preventing the industrious, enterprising, but perhaps indigent mechanic, from following his trade to advantage, or from following it at all.*

In 1833 a mechanic declared:

It cannot but strike every reflecting and observing man that a spirit unfriendly to the standing and pursuits of mechanics is fast gaining ground in this country . . . the result of which if not stopped in its onward course will be to bring them to a state of servitude less enviable than that of the vassals of the feudal lords and princes—because they may hold the name but lose the rights of freemen.

Similarly, a journeyman shoemaker complained that the shoe manufacturers

seem to think that the jours [journeymen] are designed for no other purpose than to be their subjects. . . . They seem to think it a disgrace to labor; that the laborer is not as good as other people. These little stuck-up, self-conceited individuals who have a little second-hand credit. . . . You must do as they wish . . . or you are out of their books; they have no more employment for you.

Skilled craftsmen organized trade unions, working-men's political parties, and prolabor newspapers such as the *New York Working Man's Advocate.* They demanded both long-range reforms, including social respect and free public education, and specific bread-and-butter issues—higher wages and shorter hours. Yearly, labor activities became more militant. As one New York union leader proclaimed in 1833:

The time has now arrived for the mechanics of our city to arise in their strength and determine that they will no longer submit to the thraldom which they have patiently borne for many years, nor suffer employers to appropriate an undue share of the avails of the labourer to his disadvantage.

A recognition of the antagonistic nature of the employee-employer relationship affected almost all workers by the mid-1830s. More than 200 trade unions flourished, with an estimated membership of anywhere from

100,000 to 300,000. Over 160 strikes occurred between 1833 and 1837, most of which were for higher wages. Noting the mounting evidence of class strife, the *Philadelphia Public Ledger* of October 11, 1837, looked back upon a time

not far distant, when he heard nothing from American presses, about classes and distinctions of rank. Then, all occupations were considered equally honorably, and distinctions between individuals were founded, not in trades and professions, but in character and conduct.

The relationship between labor and capital was further strained by the hostile reactions of employers and much of the middle-class public to organized workers. Employers' associations were formed to bar from employment "any man who is known to be a member of . . . any society which has for its object the direction of terms or prices for which workmen shall engage themselves."

Another frequently used managerial tactic (one which has been employed through much of this nation's history) was to persuade the public that unions were un-American and therefore undesirable. Unions, claimed the probusiness *New York Commercial Advertiser* in 1836, "are based upon the same principles as the pernicious Trade Unions in England, and in almost every case, we are informed, they are managed and controlled by foreigners."

Also effective in blocking unions were the conservative courts. English common law traditionally held that whenever two or more persons conspired to do something jointly, even when an individual was entitled to take such an action, the public interest was endangered and therefore the action was an illegal conspiracy. American courts applied this common-law definition of conspiracy to mean that any combination of workers who aimed to raise their wages or shorten their hours through united action was illegal.

One of the most noted conspiracy trials involved a group of striking journeymen tailors in New York City who were arrested and found guilty in June 1836 of entering "into a confederacy with a view of controlling others." Philip Hone, a wealthy, fashionable, and conservative New Yorker, described with approval the sentencing of the tailors. Hone's diary entry for the day of the sentencing shows the type of prejudice that workers faced:

June 6.—*In corroboration of the spirit of faction and contempt of the laws which pervades the community at this time is the conduct of the journeymen tailors, instigated by a set of vile foreigners (principally English), who, unable to endure the restraints of wholesome law well administered in their own country, take refuge here, establish trades-unions, and vilify Yankee judges and juries. Twenty odd of these were convicted at the Oyer and Terminer court* [New York Superior Criminal Court] *of a conspiracy to raise their wages and to prevent any of the craft from working at prices less than those for which they struck.*

While Hone and other businessmen were pleased with the verdict against the tailors, workers were outraged. In the week that elapsed between the verdict and the sentencing, preparations were made for massive protests. A leaflet decorated with coffins was circulated; it called workingmen to attend court on the day the tailors were to be sentenced:

On Monday, June 6, 1836, these Freemen [the tailors] are to receive their sentence, to gratify the hellish appetites of the Aristocracy. On Monday, the Liberty of the Workingmen will be interred! Judge Edwards is to chant the Requiem! Go! Go! every Freeman, every Workingman, and hear the melancholy sound of the earth on the Coffin of Equality!

The appeal of the unionists was stated in distinctly class-conscious terms. The circular went on to proclaim:

The Rich Against the Poor

Judge Edwards, the tool of the aristocracy, against the people! Mechanics and Workingmen! A deadly blow has been struck at your Liberty! . . . The Freemen of the North are now on the level with the slaves of the South! With no other privileges than laboring, that drones may fatten on your life-blood! Twenty of your brethren have been found guilty for presuming to resist a reduction of their wages! And Judge Edwards has charged an American jury, and, agreeably to that charge, they have established the precedent that workingmen have no right to regulate the price of labor, or, in other words, the rich are the only judges of the wants of the poor man.

Despite protests, the tailors were fined and the strike was broken. All in all, the gains of organized labor were slight and in the long run illusory, because not only

The Castle of Dromore

Bring no ill will to hinder us,
   My helpless babe and me,
Dread spirits of the black water,
   Clanowen's wild banshee;
And holy Mary pitying us,
   In heaven for grace that is true,
Singing hushabye, lullabye, lou lo lan,
   Sing hushabye lou lo lan.

Take time to thrive my ray of hope,
   In the garden of Dromore,
Take heed young eaglet that thy wings,
   Are feathered fit to soar.
A little rest, and then the world
   Is full of work to do,
Singing hushabye, lullabye, lou lo lan,
   Sing hushabye lou lo lan.

employers but general economic trends also undermined labor's position.

To make matters worse, the prosperous conditions that had buoyed up the Jacksonian labor movement came to an abrupt end in the depression of 1837 which lasted through the early 1840s. The hardships suffered by workers during the depression years were severe. In his *Recollections*, the humanitarian newspaper editor Horace Greeley wrote of the early effects of the depression in New York City:

the winter of 1837–38, though happily mild and open till far into January, was one of pervading destitution and suffering in our city, from paralysis of business and consequent dearth of employment. The liberality of those who could give was heavily taxed to save from famishing the tens of thousands who being needy and unable to find employment, first ran into debt so far as they could, and thenceforth must be helped or starve.

One source estimated that by January 1838, some 50,000 persons were unemployed in New York City alone. Another 200,000, it was said, were living "in utter and hopeless distress with no means of surviving the winter but those provided by charity."

Under such circumstances organized labor collapsed, leaving both skilled and unskilled workers without effective organizations at a time when increased immigration and continued industrial expansion depressed the entire wage-earning class and widened the gap between classes. As Orestes Brownson pointed out in 1840:

The actual condition of the workingman to-day is not so good as it was fifty years ago. . . . Fifty years ago, health and industrious habits, constituted no mean stock in trade, and with them almost any man might aspire to competence and independence. But it is so no longer. The wilderness has receded and already the new lands are beyond the reach of the mere laborer, and the employer has him at his mercy.

By the time Brownson wrote the above, it was becoming clear to a growing number of working men, women, and children that the industrial revolution, which had promised to liberate man, had for them only succeeded in creating a new bondage. For the workers the price of industrialization was increasing social stratification, alienation, and exploitation. Benevolent capitalism, as first conceived at Lowell, had rapidly become a contradiction of terms.

▪4▪

PARTIES, POLITICS, AND DEMOCRACY

There has been a mix-up of all the old parties and today it would be impossible to say what is the political belief of those who support the administration, or of those who attack it. . . . There are no parties properly so called, opposed one to the other and adopting a contrary political faith.

Nicholas Biddle (1831)

In the 1820s and 1830s the modern American two-party political system was born. Following the breakup of the old Federalist party in the years immediately after the War of 1812, the Republican party split to form two new parties—the Democrats and the National Republicans (renamed the Whigs in the early 1830s). During these years the last restrictions on adult white male suffrage were removed by the states. The result was the development of new political tactics aimed at appealing to the common man. Political battles became sharply contested. Fiery, emotional rhetoric replaced rational deliberation as both parties bid for mass support. As might be expected, close political contests stimulated voter interest. Political participation increased, giving the appearance that democracy was also growing.

When one looks at the problems generated by the rapid economic growth and social change during these decades, however, it becomes evident that the political parties did not really deal democratically or effectively with the people's economic and social problems. The politics of the period, then, was paradoxical. On the surface, at least, it appeared to many people as if the common man was in the ascendency and that true democracy had triumphed. Yet in retrospect, when one examines the economic, social, and moral issues of the era, both political parties appear to be conservative and either unable or unwilling to bring about the political changes necessary to cope with the nation's problems.

Andrew Jackson exemplified the new political order. Elected to the presidency in 1828, he was the first president who claimed to represent all the people. His first inauguration in March 1829 set the new tone of popular politics. A witness to the crowds on that inaugural day, Mrs. Margaret Bayard Smith, gave the following description:

The Majesty of the People [Jackson] had disappeared, . . . leaving a rabble, a mob, of boys, negros, women, children scrambling, fighting, romping. What a pity what a pity! No arrangements had been made, no police officers placed on duty and the whole house [the White House] had been inundated by the rabble mob. . . . The President, after having been literally nearly pressed to death and almost suffocated and torn to pieces by the people in their eagerness to shake hands with Old Hickory [Jackson], had retreated through the back way . . . and had escaped to his lodgings at Gadsby's [a Washington hotel]. Cut glass and china to the amount of several

*White House party celebrating the
inauguration of Andrew Jackson.*

thousand dollars had been broken in the struggle to get the refreshments, punch and other articles had been carried out in tubs and buckets, but had it been in hogsheads it would have been insufficient, ice-creams, and cake and lemonade, for 20,000 people, for it is said that number were there. . . . Ladies fainted, men were seen with bloody noses and such a scene of confusion took place as is impossible to describe—those who got in could not get out by the door again, but had to scramble out of windows.

Did this surging mob represent the triumphant common man? Some people thought so. William M. Holland was such an individual. Writing about General Jackson in an 1835 semiauthorized biography of Martin Van Buren, Jackson's friend and successor, Holland argued that the president and the people were as one.

The democratic usage, of selecting those men for office who will faithfully express the will of the people, . . . is illustrated in the example of General Jackson. The leading measures of his administration have been ardently approved by the democracy. . . .

The true cause of the surprising harmony which exists between the President and the people, is either not understood by the anti-democratic party or is misrepresented. The truth is, that the President has been sustained in his measures, because they have all been based upon a careful observation, and a thorough knowledge, of the popular will. The President has had the sagacity to observe the sentiments of the great body of the people and the integrity and firmness to carry them into effect. He has collected and embodied the wishes of the people;

he has seemed to lead public opinion, it has been because he is endowed with a penetration which has enabled him to foresee its current, and by throwing himself at its head, to bring its full force to sustain him. Guided by the fundamental principle, that the will of the majority should, in all cases, control, he has never attempted to defeat that will. He has earnestly endeavored to ascertain the wishes of his constituents, and having ascertained them, he has labored, with astonishing firmness, vigor and capacity, to carry them into effect. This is the source of that attachment which binds the heart of every true republican to the great political father of the democracy. Many a plain farmer or mechanic . . . sees that the President has reasoned as he is reasoning, but with greater rapidity and vigor; he feels that the breast of the President beats in unison with his own; that he is truly one of the people, identical in his wishes and feelings with the plain farmer at the plough.

Holland's favorable assessment of Jackson was shared by most of Old Hickory's loyal supporters. Many Jacksonians believed that the party divisions of the 1830s were a continuation of conflicts dating back to the days before the Revolution. As a Massachusetts Democratic party leader stated in 1834:

It was first Tory, then Federalist, then no party, then amalgamation, then National Republican, now Whig, and the next name they assume perhaps will be republican. . . . But by whatever name they reorganize themselves, the true democracy of the country, the producing classes, ought to be able to distinguish the enemy. . . . They are composed in general of all those who are, or who believe themselves to be favored by some adventitious circumstances of fortune. They are those . . . who have contrived to live without labor, or who hope one day to do so, and must consequently live on the labor of others.

The opponents of the Jacksonian Democrats, however, did not accept the picture of themselves as the party of privilege. At first those opposed to President Jackson formed a loose coalition known as the National Republicans. They were united mainly in their common hatred of General Jackson. But by the mid-1830s, under the new name of Whigs, these opposition forces had come to form a well-organized party able to contest the Democrats with some success.

Under the able leadership of two of the most noted senators in American history, Daniel Webster and Henry Clay, the Whigs attacked Jackson as a demagogue who had overextended his executive authority.

As president, Jackson was convinced that he, more than any other elected official, stood for the will of the people. Even before his elevation to the White House, Jackson had stated that "if I am elected to fill the Presidential chair it must be by the people; and I will be the President of the nation, and not of a party." During his two terms as president (1829–1837), Jackson acted on the assumption that he *was* the people's voice. In their name he vetoed more measures than all previous presidents combined; he also took a strong stand against the attempted nullification of a federal tariff by the state of South Carolina; finally, he implemented an aggressive Indian policy by executive proclamation, and, in one case, even in defiance of the Supreme Court. All of these

Andrew Jackson, watercolor on ivory by Anna Claypoole Peale.

measures served to greatly increase presidential power. For good or ill, the vast authority possessed by the Chief Executive today owes a great deal to Andrew Jackson.

But to his Whig opponents, Jackson's actions represented an unconstitutional usurpation of congressional rights. The strength of President Jackson, proclaimed Henry Clay in an 1837 Senate speech,

> is felt from one extremity to the other of this vast republic. By means of principles which he has introduced and innovations which he has made in our institutions, . . . he exercises uncontrolled the power of the State. . . . He has swept over the Government, during the last eight years, like a tropical tornado. Every department exhibits traces of the ravages of the storm.

The Whigs developed the theory that their party had been organized, in the words of an 1844 pamphleteer, to protect "this nation and its posterity against the imperious claims and mischievous precedents made and established by General Jackson and his partisans, to the enlargement of Executive and the diminution of Legislative power."

The fundamental principle of the Whigs, this writer emphasized, was

> the assertion of the Representative Privilege against the Executive Prerogative. No candid and sincere lover of rational, republican liberty . . . can contemplate the encroachments of Executive power . . . without a resolute revolt in his heart against that whole system of political domination by which these encroachments have been compassed.

If one were to conclude on the basis of the preceding

statements that the two parties represented different principles and policies, he would be partly correct. Although historians disagree as to just how much parties differed, most would agree that the Jacksonians had a somewhat greater appeal to the common man than did the Whigs, while the latter had greater backing among men of wealth than did the Democrats.

In addition to the specific disagreement over the nature of the presidency, Democrats and Whigs divided over banking policy and federal spending for the construction of turnpikes, canals, railways, and other internal improvements. In general, the Democrats favored free enterprise in which the federal government did not take an active part. This philosophy explains Jackson's destruction of the federally chartered Bank of the United States and his veto of a proposed highway that would have been built with federal funds.

The Whigs, on the other hand, viewed the United States as an underdeveloped country in need of government aid to the economy in the form of protective tariffs for industry, internal improvements for commerce, and a national bank to facilitate business generally.

Such differences can be exaggerated, however. Both parties, after all, appealed to about half of the electorate. The Democrats won the presidency in 1828, 1832, 1836, and 1844; the Whigs, in 1840 and 1848. Most elections were quite close, and each party attempted to gain the support of as many voters as possible. This generally meant avoiding clear-cut ideological stands on basic issues, unless the overwhelming majority favored such a stand. Instead of running on a well-thought-out platform, most politicians of both parties made emotional appeals to the voters. Candidates were put up because of their

Andrew Jackson, commemorative ribbon.

popular appeal. Thus, Jackson, already famous as the military hero of the Battle of New Orleans, made an excellent choice. Similarly, the two successful Whig candidates, William Henry Harrison in 1840 and Zachary Taylor in 1848, were both heroic military generals.

Symbols became important in politics. The hickory tree, a symbol of Jackson's nickname, Old Hickory, was used by the Democrats. The most successful Whig symbol was the log cabin which they displayed in 1840 to indicate that their candidate had been raised in a cabin and therefore was a man of the people.

Parades, picnics, slogans, and songs all proved helpful in winning voters. During the early 1830s, Jacksonians marched to rallies in New York City where they were trying to gain the support of the working men. To the old tune of "Yankee Doodle" they sang:

> Mechanics, Carters, Laborers
> Must form a close connection,
> And show the rich Aristocrats
> Their powers, at this election.

> Yankee Doodle, smoke 'em out,
> The proud, the banking faction.
> None but such as Hartford Feds*
> Oppose the poor and Jackson.

In 1840, Martin Van Buren, the Democratic presidential incumbent, was attacked as an aristocrat, living luxuriously in the White House at the people's expense. A popular Whig campaign song went:

---

* "Hartford Feds" refers to New England Federalists who had met in Hartford during the War of 1812 and discussed possible disunion.

Let Van from his coolers of silver drink wine,
  And lounge on his cushioned setee,
Our man on a buckeye bench can recline,
  Content with hard cider is he.

A good example of the effective political campaigner was Colonel Davy Crockett, the Tennessee frontiersman who was a legend even in his own lifetime. When first in politics, Crockett had been a Jacksonian Democrat, but in the early 1830s he switched his allegiance to the Whigs. Issues had nothing to do with his change. The following passage from Crockett's autobiography gives a good picture of how the successful politician won popular support. It describes the time when Davy first entered a political campaign in Tennessee.

I went first into Heckman county, to see what I could do among the people as a candidate. Here they told me that they wanted to move their town nearer to the centre of the county, and I must come out in favor of it. There's no devil if I knowed what this meant, or how the town was to be moved; and so I kept dark, going on the identical same plan that I now find is called "non-committal." About this time there was a great squirrel hunt on Duck river, which was among my people. They were to hunt two days; then to meet and count the scalps, and have a big barbecue, and what might be called a tip-top country frolic. The dinner, and a general treat, was all to be paid for by the party having taken the fewest scalps. I joined one side, taking the place of one of the hunters, and got a gun ready for the hunt. I killed a great many squirrels, and when we counted scalps, my party was victorious.

The company had every thing to eat and drink that could be furnished in so new a country, and much fun and good humor prevailed. But before the regular frolic commenced, I mean the dancing, I was called on to make a speech as a candidate; which was business I was . . . ignorant of.

A public document I had never seen, nor did I know there were such things; and how to begin I couldn't tell. I made many apologies, and tried to get off, for I know'd I had a man to run against who could speak prime, and I know'd too, that I wasn't able to shuffle and cut with him. He was there, and knowing my ignorance as well as I did myself, he also urged me to make a speech. The truth is, he thought my being a candidate was a mere matter of sport; and didn't think for a moment, that he was in any danger from an ignorant backwoods bear hunter. But I found I couldn't get off, and so I determined just to go ahead, and leave it to chance what I should say. I got up and told the people I reconed they know'd what I had come for, but if not, I could tell them. I had come for their votes, and if they didn't watch mighty close I'd get them too. But worst of all was, that I could not tell them anything about government. I tried to speak about something, and I cared very little what, until I choaked up as bad as if my mouth had been jamm'd and cramm'd chock full of dry mush. There the people stood, listening all the while, with their eyes, mouths, and ears all open, to catch every word I would speak.

At last I told them I was like a fellow I had heard of not long before. He was beating on the head of an empty barrel near the roadside, when a traveler, who was passing along, asked him what he was doing that for? The fellow replied that there was some cider in that barrel a few days before, and he was trying to see if there was any then, but if there was he couldn't get at it. I told them that there had been a little bit of a speech in me a while ago, but I believed I couldn't get it out. They all roared out in a mighty laugh, and I told some other anecdotes, equally amusing to them, and believing I had them in a first-rate way, I quit and got down, thanking the people for their attention. But I took care to remark that I was as dry as a powder-horn, and that I thought it was time for us all to wet our whistles a little: and so I put off to the liquor stand, and was followed by the greater part of the crowd.

I felt certain this was necessary, for I knowed my competitor could talk government matters to them as easy as he pleased. He had, however, mighty few left to hear him, as I continued with the crowd, now and then taking a horn, and telling good-humored stories, till he was done speaking. I found I was good for the votes at the hunt. . . .

But to cut this matter short, I was elected, doubling my competitor, and nine votes over.

The truth was that for most politicians victory at the polls was more important than policies or principles. One of the major reasons that party politicians put so much emphasis on winning elections was that once in office they could appoint many of their friends and followers to nonelective offices. This was known as the spoils system. As a New York Democrat, William Marcy, stated: triumphant politicians "claim as a matter of right the advantages of success. They see nothing wrong in the rule, that to the victors belong the spoils of the enemy." Jobs such as postmen, government clerks, revenue officials, tariff collectors, ambassadors, and cabinet ministers were all filled by loyal members of the political party in power.

While the fanfare of campaigns and the promises of patronage generated a good deal of political excitement among the people, there were others who would have preferred the politicians and their parties to be more principled and more concerned with basic issues. Stephen Simpson was such a person. A Philadelphia labor leader, Simpson published *The Working Man's Manual* in 1831. This work sharply criticized the existing party system.

Nothing of a public nature, at the present era, is so worthy of the attention of the people as the . . . parties now in vogue [who are] neither advancing the good of the nation nor the prosperity of her citizens, but blindly ministering to the avarice, ambition, or pride of some temporary idol, who is worshipped one day and immolated on the next. A party grafted purely on principle has never yet engrossed the ardent people of this excited country.

People supported such unscrupulous parties, Simpson concluded, because they were enticed

by demagogues to the detriment of their best interests, the sacrifice of their time, and the loss of their character. Lured on by the cant of party, the slang of affected patriotism, and the hollow promise of patronage, men have closed their eyes as well as their understandings to the deception of the game, which made use of them and

The election of 1840, Whig headquarters.

their interests for the sheer and exclusive benefit of an aspiring demagogue.

Less radical writers than Simpson made similar evaluations of the American party system in the Jacksonian era. Alexis de Tocqueville, the brilliant Frenchman, after observing the political parties in the United States analyzed their nature in one of his notebooks. He made a distinction between what he termed "great" parties and "small" parties. Great parties were "those concerned with principles and not their consequences, with general questions and not with particular cases, with ideas and not men." The small parties, on the other hand, were "without political faith, their characters are consistent and stamped with a blatant selfishness shown in all their acts. . . . Their language is violent, their progress timid and uncertain. The means they employ are wretched, as is the end they seek."

Tocqueville believed from his study of American history that the Federalists and Jeffersonian Republicans had been "great" parties. But those of Jackson's time were decidedly not.

In the whole world I do not see a more wretched and shameful sight than that presented by the different coteries (they do not deserve the name of parties) which now divide the Union. In broad daylight one sees all the petty, shameful passions disturbing them which generally one is careful to keep hidden at the bottom of the human heart. As for the interest of the country, no one thinks about it, and if one talks about it that is just for form's sake. . . .

It is pitiful to see what a deluge of coarse insults,

what petty slander and what gross calumnies, fill the newspapers that serve as organs for the parties, and with what shameful disregard of social decencies they daily drag before the tribunal of public opinion the honour of families and the secrets of the domestic hearth.

Looking back on the Jacksonian period from the perspective of the present, there appears to be much validity in Simpson's and Tocqueville's criticisms of political parties. The politicians, concerned with winning elections, flattered the common man with greater and greater frequency. This in turn helped stimulate increased political interest and participation. Traditionally historians in studying the campaign rhetoric extolling the virtues of the people, and seeing the growth of political participation, assumed that this period marked a major advance for democracy. Yet it now seems clear that neither of the two major parties offered voters what could truly be called a democratic choice. Both Whigs and Democrats were essentially conservative.

This conservatism becomes apparent when one looks at the major issues of the time and the way in which the two parties dealt with them. Several major issues existed in Jacksonian America. These would include the industrialization and economic growth of the nation with the already apparent tendencies toward concentration and exploitation, slavery, the treatment of minority groups and the less fortunate, and the extent and quality of public education. Yet the issues that engaged the two major parties—tariffs, banking, Indian and land policy, the spoils system, and internal improvements—either were not the most significant ones or, when they touched on major problems, they did so in an ineffectual or even negative manner.

Slavery is a good example. No more pressing problem faced the young nation than the holding of millions of blacks in bondage. Nothing was more obviously inconsistent with the Declaration of Independence or with the democratic philosophy that Americans proclaimed on the Fourth of July and other occasions. But because of the nature of two-party politics both Whigs and Democrats tried to avoid the issue of slavery. They were concerned about building national parties and did not wish to bring up an issue that threatened to divide the country and endanger the newly established political coalitions.

When the abolitionists pushed the slavery question to the fore in the mid-1830s through widespread dissemination of antislavery literature by mail and petitions to Congress, the government tried to silence antislavery sentiment. Jackson's postmaster general, Amos Kendall, in 1835 encouraged postal officials to confiscate abolitionist mails.

It was right [Kendall claimed] *to propose to the Anti-Slavery Society voluntarily to desist from attempting to send their publications into Southern States by public mails; and their refusal to do so, after they were apprised that the entire mails were put in jeopardy by them, is but another evidence of the fatuity of the counsels by which they are directed. . . . .*

Postmasters may lawfully know in all cases the contents of newspapers, because the law expressly provides that they shall be so put up that they may be readily examined; and if they know those contents to be calculated and designed to produce the commission of the most aggravated crimes upon the property and persons of their fellow citizens, it cannot be doubted that it is their duty to detain them, if not even to hand them over to civil authorities.

In this opinion of the postmaster general, President Jackson, himself a slaveholder, was in complete agreement. On one occasion Jackson called abolitionism a "wicked plan of inciting the negroes to insurrection and massacre." Congress made no objection, and the following year (1836), in clear violation of the Bill of Rights, adopted the so-called Gag Rule by refusing to accept or read abolitionist petitions. In short, national politics was dominated by proslavery sentiment.

The failure of the two major parties to confront basic issues, or to do so in a less than democratic manner, helps explain the extensive organized activity outside the two-party system. There were widespread demands for social and economic change; but, since established political institutions discouraged innovation, persons seeking change felt forced to create new channels.

The reformers of the age understood that the maintenance of basic liberties could not be left in the hands of the politicians. As Wendell Phillips, one of the most brilliant abolitionists, wrote:

Republics exist only on the tenure of being constantly agitated. The antislavery agitation is an important, nay, an essential part of the machinery of the state. It is not a disease nor a medicine. No; it is the normal state—the normal state of the nation. Never, to our latest posterity, can we afford to do without prophets, like [William Lloyd] Garrison, to stir up the monotony of wealth, and reawake the people to the great ideas that are constantly fading out of their minds—to trouble the waters, that there may be health in their flow. Every government is always growing corrupt. Every Secretary of state is . . . an enemy to the people, of necessity, because the moment he joins the government, he gravitates against that popular agitation which is the life of a republic. . . . The republic that sinks to sleep, trusting to constitutions and machinery, to politicians and statesmen, for the safety of its liberties, never will have any. The people are to be waked to a new effort, just as the Church has to be regenerated in each age. The anti-slavery agitation is a necessity of each age, to keep ever on the alert this faithful vigilance, so constantly in danger of sleep.

The so-called democracy of the Jacksonian era, then, was a relative thing. More people were participating in politics than in previous periods, and politicians of both major parties claimed to represent "the people." Yet real changes in the quality of American life were slow in coming through political channels. Fortunately, agitators such as Wendell Phillips and William Lloyd Garrison did exist; in the long run such persons were able to push the politicians in a more humane direction.

∎5∎

JIM CROW NORTH

The prejudice of race appears to be stronger in the states that have abolished slavery than in those where it still exists; and nowhere is it so intolerant as in those states where servitude has never been known. . . . The Negro is free, but he can share neither the rights, nor the pleasures, nor the labor, nor the afflictions, nor the tomb of him whose equal he has been declared to be; and he cannot meet him upon fair terms in life or in death.

Alexis de Tocqueville (1835)

There has never been a Mason-Dixon line on racial questions in America. Even during the heyday of abolitionist agitation, the overwhelming majority of white Americans —northerners and southerners—believed the Negro to be a biologically inferior being, unfit for equal status with whites.

Northern racial discrimination was blatant. The free black was denied a political and legal voice, segregated socially, and kept at the lowest economic level. So prescribed was the life of the Negro in the free states that some blacks found it comparable to slavery itself. Such a comparison was made by Martin R. Delany, an active abolitionist and black nationalist. Writing on the "Comparative Condition of the Colored People of the United States," Delany claimed that the freemen

in the non-slaveholding States, occupy the very same position politically, religiously, civilly and socially, (with but few exceptions), as the bondman [slave] occupies in the slave States.

In those States, the bondman is disfranchised, and for the most part so are we. He is denied all civil, religious, and social privileges, except such as he gets by mere sufferance, and so are we. They have no part nor lot in the government of the country, neither have we. They are ruled and governed without representation, existing as mere nonentities among the citizens, and excrescences on the body politic—a mere dreg in community, and so are we. Where then is our political superiority to the enslaved? None, neither are we superior in any other relation to society, except that we are de facto masters of ourselves and joint rulers of our own domestic household, while the bondman's self is claimed by another, and his relation to his family denied him. What the unfortunate classes are in Europe, such are we in the United States, which is folly to deny, insanity not to understand, blindness not to see, and surely now full time that our eyes were opened to these startling truths, which for ages have stared us full in the face.

Even what little freedom did exist for northern Negroes could sometimes be lost. The story of Solomon Northup well illustrates this. Northup was a free black living in Saratoga Springs, New York, where he did various jobs for whites during the summer season at that fashionable resort town. He was a married man with three children; he was also well read and an accomplished violinist. One day in late March of 1841, two men approached him on the streets of Saratoga. They told him that they were with a circus company and, in Northup's words,

that they had found much difficulty in procuring music for their entertainments, and that if I would accompany them as far as New-York, they would give me one dollar for each day's services, and three dollars in addition for every night I played [the violin] at their performances, besides sufficient to pay the expenses of my return from New-York to Saratoga.

Being without work at the time, Northup accepted their offer and accompanied the two men to New York where he was then informed that the circus was in Washington, D.C. Taking the precaution to procure papers in New York that indicated he was a free man, Northup went with the two men to the nation's capitol. There, however, he was plied with liquor and possibly drugged. He awoke in the night feeling very ill, and, in his words,

conscious of some one entering my room. There seemed to be several—a mingling of various voices—but how many, or who they were, I cannot tell. . . . I only remember, with any degree of distinctness, that I was told it was necessary to go to a physician and procure medicine, and that pulling on my boots, without coat or hat, I followed them through a long passage-way, or alley, into the open street. . . . From that moment I was insensible. How long I remained in that condition . . . I do not know; but when consciousness returned, I found myself alone, in utter darkness, and in chains.

The pain in my head had subsided in a measure, but I was very faint and weak. I was setting upon a low bench, made of rough boards. . . . I was hand-cuffed. Around my ankles were a pair of heavy fetters. One end of a chain was fastened to a large ring in the floor, the other to the fetters on my ankles. I tried in vain to stand upon my feet. Waking from such a painful trance, it was some time before I could collect my thoughts. Where was I? What was the meaning of these chains? . . . What had I done to deserve imprisonment in such a dungeon? I could not comprehend. . . . I felt of my pockets, so far as the fetters would allow—far enough, indeed, to ascertain that I had not only been robbed of liberty, but that my money and free papers were also gone! Then did the idea begin to break upon my mind, at first dim and confused, that I had been kidnapped. But that thought was incredible. There must have been . . . some unfortunate mistake. It could not be that a free citizen of New-York, who had wronged no man, nor violated any law, should be dealt with this inhumanly. The more I contemplated my situation, however, the more I became confirmed in my suspicions. It was a desolate thought, indeed. I felt there was no trust or mercy in unfeeling man; and commending myself to the God of the oppressed, bowed my head upon my fettered hands, and wept most bitterly.

Northup's worst fears were soon confirmed. He learned that he was imprisoned in a slave pen. Northup recalled,

Strange as it may seem within plain sight of this same house, looking down from its commanding height upon it, was the Capitol. The voices of patriotic representatives boasting of freedom and equality, and the rattling of the poor slave's chains, almost commingled. A slave pen within the very shadow of the capitol.

Northup inquired of his captor, a slave trader named James Burch, the cause of his imprisonment.

He [Burch] answered that I was his slave—that he had bought me, and that he was about to send me to New-Orleans. I asserted, aloud and boldly, that I was a free man—a resident of Saratoga, where I had a wife and children, who were also free, and that my name was North-up. I complained bitterly of the strange treatment I had received, and threatened, upon my liberation, to have satisfaction for the wrong. He denied that I was free, and with an emphatic oath, declared that I came from Georgia. Again and again I asserted I was no man's slave, and insisted upon his taking off my chains at once. He endeavored to hush me, as if he feared my voice would be overheard. But I would not be silent, and denounced the authors of my imprisonment, whoever they might be, as unmitigated villains. Finding he could not quiet me, he flew into a towering passion. With blasphemous oaths, he called me a black liar, a runaway from Georgia, and every other profane and vulgar epithet that the most indecent fancy could conceive.

Turning to his assistant, one Ebenezer Radburn, Burch "ordered the paddle and cat-o'-nine-tails to be brought in."

The paddle . . . was a piece of hardwood board, eighteen or twenty inches long, moulded to the shape of an . . . ordinary oar. The flattened portion, which was about the size in circumference of two open hands, was bored

Sold Off to Georgy

Slow (♩. = 44)

Fare-well, fel-low serv-ants, O-ho! O-ho! I'm gwine 'way to leave you O-ho! O-ho! I'm gwine to leave de ole coun-try, O-

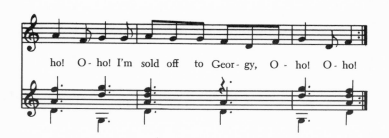

ho! O - ho! I'm sold off to Geor - gy, O - ho! O - ho!

My dear wife and one child,
   Oho! Oho!
My poor heart is breaking,
   Oho! Oho!
No more shall I see you
   Oho! Oho!
Oh, no more for ever.
   Oho! Oho!

with a small auger in numerous places. The cat was a large rope of many strands—the strands unraveled, and a knot tied at the extremity of each.

As soon as these formidable weapons appeared, I was seized by both of them, and roughly divested of my clothing. My feet . . . were fastened to the floor. Drawing me over the bench, face downwards, Radburn placed his heavy foot upon the fetters, between my wrists, holding them painfully to the floor. With the paddle, Burch commenced beating me. Blow after blow was inflicted upon my naked body. When his unrelenting arm grew tired, he stopped and asked if I still insisted I was a free man. I did insist upon it, and then the blows were renewed, faster and more energetically, if possible, than before. When again tired, he would repeat the same question, and receiving the same answer, continue his cruel labor. All this time, the incarnate devil was uttering most fiendish oaths. At length the paddle broke, leaving the useless handle in his hand. Still I would not yield. All his brutal blows could not force from my lips the foul lie that I was a slave. Casting madly on the floor the handle of the broken paddle, he seized the rope. This was far more painful than the other. I struggled with all my power, but it was in vain. I prayed for mercy, but my prayer was only answered with imprecations and with stripes. I thought I must die beneath the lashes of the accursed brute. Even now the flesh crawls upon my bones, as I recall the scene. I was all on fire. My sufferings I can compare to nothing else than the burning agonies of hell!

Beaten senseless, Northup was then shipped to New Orleans and sold into slavery. For twelve years he bitterly endured the loss of freedom, until, through good fortune, his plight became known to an influential and sympathetic white man from his home state of New York who intervened to secure his freedom and reunite him with his family.

Such an experience was not unique. As Northup concludes in the narrative recalling his experiences, *Twelve Years a Slave:* "I doubt not hundreds have been as unfortunate as myself; that hundreds of free citizens have been kidnapped and sold into slavery, and are at this moment wearing out their lives on plantations in Texas and Louisiana."

Slavery itself, of course, had not always been limited to the South. At the time of the Revolution it existed throughout the country, and although the northern states all abolished slavery in the first decades following independence, a few northern slaves still were held in bondage as late as 1827.

But more importantly, the long slave past had conditioned whites to regard blacks as inferiors. This attitude did not change with emancipation. As one writer observed, the abolishment of slavery in the North did not bring true freedom, "chains of a stronger kind still manacled their limbs, from which no legislative act could free them; a mental and moral subordination and inferiority, to which tyrant custom has here subjected all the sons and daughters of Africa."

The legal and political position of free northern blacks was dictated by white prejudice. Though free in the theoretical sense of having the right to life, liberty, and property, freedom for blacks did not carry with it other usual rights of citizenship. In fact, before the law Ne-

Kidnapping free blacks.

groes were seldom regarded as citizens. An English visitor, William Chambers, noted this:

The federal constitution is silent about race or colour, but interpreting it, American lawgivers arrive at the conclusion, that the United States are the property of whites, and that persons with a tinge of dark colour in their countenance, though born free, are not citizens. . . . There seems, in short, to be a fixed notion throughout the whole of the states, whether slave or free, that the coloured is by nature a subordinate race; and that in no circumstances, can it be considered equal to the whites.

Not only was the Negro denied citizenship, but also in several northern states political rights once enjoyed were taken away. One of the cruelest ironies was that the very democratic reforms which extended white political democracy in the 1820s and 1830s actually reduced Negro rights. This was particularly true of suffrage reform. In New York, New Jersey, Connecticut, and Pennsylvania, where Negroes had voted previously, new constitutions, granting white manhood suffrage, virtually disfranchised the black. By 1840, only in northern New England, where few blacks lived, was suffrage not racially restricted. An estimated 93 percent of the northern free Negro population was effectively barred from the polls.

Racial discrimination in the courtroom was even more severe. During the Jacksonian period no Negroes served on juries. In five northern states blacks were prohibited from testifying in court cases where a white man was a party. Under such circumstances the courts further bent the law to favor whites. As a New Yorker observed in the 1840s:

It is hardly possible that persons in their condition [Negroes] should have an impartial trial. Hated, trodden down, and despised, they had not the means to procure counsel and defend themselves against false and malicious charges, and false witnesses; and too often, an accusation against them was equivalent to conviction.

Excluded from politics and discriminated against by white justice and law, many Negroes and their white sympathizers looked to education as a key to advancing the race. As a Negro national convention resolved in 1832: "If we ever expect to see the influence of prejudice decrease and ourselves respected, it must be by the blessings of an enlightened education."

Yet in this area, as in politics, frustration and failure were frequent. Whites reacted strongly against what they thought of as an "unwholesome colored population" sharing schoolrooms with their children. And when it came to Negro demands for training in the classics (this was basic to the white student's studies), horrified whites asked, "What benefit can it be to a waiter or coachman to read Horace?"

At first blacks had difficulty finding any school willing to accept persons of color. The complaint of the first Negro newspaper, *Freedom's Journal*, in 1827, summed up the frustration of many blacks:

While the benevolence of the age has founded and endowed seminaries of Learning for all other classes and nations, we have to lament, that as yet, no door is open to receive the degraded children of Africa. Alone they

COLORED SCHOLARS EXCLUDED FROM SCHOOLS.

A *page from the* Anti-Slavery Almanac, *1839.*

have stood—alone they remain stationary; while charity extends the hands to all others.

By the 1830s, however, separate schools for black children were becoming common in most northern cities. Such schools were invariably of poorer quality than corresponding white institutions. The findings of an educational society in New York City would have been applicable to most northern cities. White students, they reported, were housed in "splendid, almost palatial edifices," while by contrast colored children were "pent up in filthy neighborhoods, in old and dilapidated buildings" and "held down to low associations and gloomy surroundings." The cause of such discrepancy was in large measure financial. In New York, for instance, the ratio of white to black students was 40 to 1, yet the ratio of educational expenditures on the two groups was a startling 1,600 to 1—$1,600 were spent on white schools for every dollar spent on schools for blacks!

While separate facilities—however inadequate—at least provided some educational opportunities for blacks, the dream of an integrated, egalitarian system of education never died. Black and white abolitionists and philanthropists tried on several occasions to establish such institutions. Yet even though the schools established were private and not dependent on the public purse, white hostility was invariably aroused—often to such an extent as to force such schools to close.

The story of Noyes Academy in Canaan, New Hampshire, is illustrative. Established by a group of abolitionists "to afford colored youth a fair opportunity to show that they are capable, equally with the whites, of improving themselves in every scientific attainment, every

COLORED SCHOOLS BROKEN UP, IN THE FREE STATES.

A *page from the* Anti-Slavery Almanac, *1839.*

social virtue, and every Christian ornament," Noyes Academy opened its doors to twenty-eight whites and fourteen Negroes in March 1835. The black students attracted to Canaan were exemplary and included several later leaders of the abolitionist movement—Henry Highland Garnet, Thomas S. Sidney, and Alexander Crummell from New York, and Thomas Paul from Boston.

At first things seemed to go well. An English traveler visiting the New Hampshire town shortly after the school opened commended what he saw as the "spirit of liberality unknown, or at least unheard of, in any other part of the Union. . . ."

Yet very soon, in the words of Crummell, "Fourteen black boys with books in their hands set the entire Granite State crazy!" Outraged by the presence of the biracial academy, Canaan residents met and announced that they "are determined to take effective measures to remove it." A mob gathered on the Fourth of July, 1835, to accomplish this object, but was dispersed by the magistrate. Later in July, however, a so-called legal Town Meeting voted to abolish the school in "the *interest* of the town, the *honor* of the State, and the *good* of the whole community, (both black and white)." On August 10 this decision was forcefully implemented. With the help of men from neighboring towns and almost a hundred teams of oxen, the academy building was ripped from its foundations. A brief meeting followed in which the abolitionists were damned while praises were shouted to the Constitution and the Revolutionary forefathers.

Actions such as that at Canaan were, unfortunately, neither uncommon nor sharply condemned by the majority of whites. A classic case of white suppression of Negro education occurred in the village of Canterbury, Connecticut, in the early 1830s. The beginning of this story was told as follows by the abolitionist William Jay:

Miss [Prudence] Crandall, a communicant in the Baptist church, and, as we believe, a lady of irreproachable character, had for some time been at the head of a female boarding school, in the town of Canterbury, Connecticut, when in the autumn of 1832 a pious colored female applied to her for admission into her school, stating that she wanted "to get a little more learning— enough, if possible, to teach colored children." After some hesitation, Miss Crandall consented to admit her, but was soon informed that this intruder must be dismissed, or that the school would be greatly injured. This threat turned her attention to the cruel prejudices and disadvantages under which the blacks are suffering, and she resolved to open a school exclusively for colored girls. . . . She discontinued her school, and in February, 1833, gave public notice of her intention to open one for colored girls. This notice excited prodigious commotion in the town of Canterbury. That black girls should presume to learn reading, and writing, and music, and geography, was past all bearing. A legal town meeting was summoned to consider the awful crisis. At this meeting resolutions were passed expressing the strongest disapprobation of the proposed school.

The resolutions of the town meeting . . . were communicated to Miss Crandall by the "civil authority and selectmen"; but that lady stood firm—she refused to retreat from the ground she had taken.

Prudence Crandall.

Other "legal" harassment soon followed, as Jay's account relates:

Among the pupils of Miss Crandall, was a colored girl about seventeen years of age, who had come from Rhode Island to enjoy the advantages of the school. The pursuit of knowledge under discouraging difficulties has rarely failed to excite applause; and the virtuous struggles of the poor and obscure to improve and elevate themselves, claim the sympathy of Christian benevolence. In the present instance, we behold a youthful female, of a despised and depressed race, attempting to emerge from the ignorance and degradation into which she had been cast by birth; and abandoning her home and friends, and travelling to another State, applying for instruction to the only seminary in the whole country open to receive her. And now let us see what sympathy this poor and defenceless, but innocent and praiseworthy girl, experienced. On the day after her arrival, she was ordered by the selectmen to leave the town. This order, as illegal as it was inhuman, was disregarded; and on the 22d April, Mr. Judson and his fellow functionaries instituted, on behalf of the town, a suit against her, under an old vagrant act of Connecticut, and a writ was issued . . . [reciting] that according to the statute she had forfeited to the town $1.62 for each day she had remained in it, since she was ordered to depart; and that in default of payment, she WAS TO BE WHIPPED ON THE NAKED BODY NOT EXCEEDING TEN STRIPES, unless she departed within ten days after conviction.

On May 24, 1833, the legislators of the State of Connecticut passed a law which prohibited the establishment of "any school, academy, or literary institution, for the instruction or education of colored persons who are not inhabitants of this state." Miss Crandall was tried under this law, and, although she was eventually freed on a technicality, the chief justice of Connecticut, David Daggett, in hearing her case ruled that Negroes were not citizens.

Not content with such "legal" obstructions, the townsmen also resorted to other types of pressure. On May 25, the day after the Connecticut law against the school, one Negro girl student wrote the following account:

There are thirteen scholars now in the school. The Canterburians are savage—they will not sell Miss Crandall an article from their shops. . . . But the happiness I enjoy here pays me for all. The place is delightful; all that is wanting to complete the scene is civilized men. Last evening the news reached us that the new Law had been passed. The bell rang, and a cannon was fired for half an hour. Where is justice? In the midst of all this Miss Crandall is unmoved. When we walk out, horns are blown and pistols fired.

In innumerable ways Miss Crandall and her students were tormented. Though they tried bravely to maintain the school, the pressures were overwhelming. The end came in September 1833. The Reverend Samuel J. May, a white abolitionist minister who had tried to help Miss Crandall, describes the sad end of the school:

About twelve o'clock, on the night of the 9th of September, Miss Crandall's house was assaulted by a number of persons with heavy clubs and iron bars; five win-

dow sashes were demolished and ninety panes of glass dashed to pieces.

I was summoned next morning to the scene of destruction and the terror-stricken family. Never before had Miss Crandall seemed to quail, and her pupils had become afraid to remain another night under her roof. The front rooms of the house were hardly tenantable; and it seemed foolish to repair them only to be destroyed again. After due consideration, therefore, it was determined that the school should be abandoned. The pupils were called together, and I was requested to announce to them our decision. Never before had I felt so deeply sensible of the cruelty of the persecution which had been carried on for eighteen months, in that New England village against a family of defenceless females. Twenty harmless, well-behaved girls, whose only offence against the peace of the community was that they had come together there to obtain useful knowledge and moral culture, were to be told that they had better go away, because . . . the house in which they dwelt would not be protected by the guardians of the town, the conservators of the peace, the officers of justice, the men of influence in the village where it was situated. The words almost blistered my lips. My bosom glowed with indignation. I felt ashamed of my country, ashamed of my color. . . .

To blacks such incidents as those at Canaan and Canterbury represented but another of the bitter ironies they faced daily. As one Negro noted in 1839:

The colored people are . . . charged with want of desire for education and improvement, yet, if a colored man comes to the door of our institutions of learning, with

The Village of Canterbury. (Prudence Crandall's house is marked with an "A.")

desires ever so strong, the lords of these institutions rise up and shut the door; and then you say we have not the desire nor the ability to acquire education. Thus, while the white youths enjoy all these advantages, we are excluded and shut out, and must remain ignorant.

As might be expected, given the nature and extent of white prejudice, discrimination was not limited to legal, political, and educational matters. For the majority of free Negroes it was most manifest in the daily struggle for economic existence. Employment opportunities were largely limited to menial, unskilled, and poorly paid jobs. It was assumed by whites that Negroes, being inferiors, were suited only for those tasks that white workers found too burdensome or socially degrading. Thus, black men could be found employed as waiters, servants, bootblacks, porters, coachmen, barbers, and common laborers; black women worked as seamstresses, servants, cooks, and washerwomen.

Since these menial positions were nearly the only ones available, Negroes took them. This in turn reinforced white beliefs that blacks were unfit for more skilled jobs or the professions.

We see them [Negroes] engaged in no business that requires even ordinary capacity, [noted a Pennsylvanian in the late 1830s] in no enterprizes requiring talents to conduct them. The mass are improvident, and seek the lowest avocations, and the most menial stations.

By the late 1830s, even the menial jobs traditionally open to Negroes were increasingly given over to whites, especially to the Irish and German immigrants coming to America in ever increasing numbers. A Negro newspaper noted in 1838:

> These impoverished and destitute beings . . . are crowding themselves into every place of business and of labor, and driving the poor colored American citizen out. Along the wharves, where the colored man once done the whole business of shipping and unshipping—in stores where his services were once rendered, and in families where the chief places were filled by him, in all these situations there are substituted foreigners or white Americans.

However destitute the new immigrants were on their arrival, they were white, and in their economic competition with Negroes this gave them unquestioned advantage. In New York City, for example, as the Irish were employed increasingly as cartmen (haulers of heavy goods with pushcarts) and porters, the authorities refused to license Negroes for these jobs on the grounds that "it would bring them [Negro cartmen and porters] into collision with white men of the same calling, and they would get their . . . carts dumped into the dock, and themselves abused and beaten."

Often the anti-Negro violence that the New York authorities warned about did occur when blacks competed with whites for the same jobs. In Philadelphia—the City of Brotherly Love—five major anti-Negro riots took place between 1832 and 1849. The most serious of these, in the summer of 1834, saw white workingmen march through the Negro section and systematically destroy homes, churches, and meeting halls, clubbing and stoning the black residents. Hundreds of Negroes were forced to flee the city.

A white citizen's committee later assessing the riot blamed it on the employment of Negroes while some whites were unemployed. To prevent such outbreaks in the future they called upon Negro leaders to impress upon their people "the necessity, as well as propriety, of behaving themselves inoffensively and with civility at all times and upon all occasions; taking care, as they pass along the streets, or assemble together, not to be obtrusive." Other northern cities witnessed similar violence.

If anything, the tensions between the races grew in the years before the Civil War as whites continued to displace Negro workers. By the 1850s Frederick Douglass, the noted Negro abolitionist, observed in a widely circulated editorial entitled "Learn Trades or Starve":

White men are becoming house-servants, cooks and stewards on vessels—at hotels. —They are becoming porters, stevedores, wood-sawyers, hod-carriers [brick carriers], white-washers and barbers, so that the blacks can scarcely find the means of subsistence—a few years ago, even a white barber would have been a curiosity—now their poles stand on every street. Formerly blacks were almost the exclusive coachmen in wealthy families: this is so no longer; white men are now employed, and for aught we see, they fill their servile station with an obsequiousness as profound as that of the blacks. The readiness and ease with which they adapt themselves to these conditions ought not be lost sight of by the colored people. The meaning is very important, and we *should learn it. We are taught our insecurity by it. Without the means of living, life is a curse, and leaves us at the mercy of the oppressor to become his debased slaves.*

Douglass asked in conclusion:

Now, colored men, what do you mean to do, for you must do something? The American Colonization Society tells you to go to Canada. Others tell you to go to school. We tell you to go to work; and to work you must go or die.

Douglass' advice—go to work—was easier said than done. Pushed out of jobs by white workers, excluded from most trade unions, seldom given a chance for apprenticeship training, the economic existence of the free Negro was a precarious one.

Added to their other burdens, northern Negroes were almost entirely segregated from whites in all aspects of life. Negroes in the North lived chiefly in the large cities where they were crowded into ghetto tenements such as "Nigger Hill" and "New Guinea" in Boston, "Little Africa" in Cincinnati, or the notorious "Five Points" section of New York. A minister gave the following description of the Five Points:

Lodging-rooms above ground are numerous in the narrow lanes, and in the dark dangerous alleys that surround the Five Points. Rooms are rented from two to ten dollars a month, into which no human being would put a dog—attics, dark as midnight at noonday, without window or door they can shut, without chimney or stove, and crowded with men, women, and little children. Chil-

dren are born in sorrow, and raised in reeking vice and bestiality, that no heathen degradation can exceed.

Segregation of blacks extended from education and housing to hotels, hospitals, theaters, churches, and even cemeteries. Special "Jim Crow" sections were provided on railways and steamboats. Racial prejudice, one observer concluded, "haunts its victim wherever he goes—in the hospitals where humanity suffers—in the churches where it kneels to God—in the prisons where it expiates its offenses—in the graveyards where it sleeps the last sleep." Charles Lyell, a noted English geologist, noticed this segregation in his American travels of the mid-1840s:

The extent to which the [northern] Americans carry their repugnance to all association with the coloured race on equal terms remained to the last an enigma to me. They feel, for example, an insurmountable objection to sit down to the same table with a well-dressed, well-informed, and well-educated man of colour, while the same persons would freely welcome one of their own race of meaner capacity and ruder manners to boon companionship. . . . If the repugnance arose from any physical causes, any natural antipathy of race, we should not see the rich Southerners employing black slaves to wait on their persons, prepare their food, nurse and suckle their white children, and live with them as mistresses. We should never see the black lady's maid sitting in the same carriage with her mistress, and supporting her when fatigued, and last, though not least, we should not meet with numerous mixed breed springing up every where from the union of the two races.

One should certainly not conclude from this, however, that the northern free Negroes were no better off than their slave brothers and sisters in the South. For, if nothing else, northern blacks were *legally free*. They could not be bought and sold, or forcibly separated from their families. They were not subject to every arbitrary whim of a master, mistress, or overseer. Furthermore, although a victim of nearly every form of racial discrimination, some opportunities for social and economic advancement did exist. Education, though largely segregated, was at least available. Even a few white colleges, notably Amherst, Bowdoin, Oneida Institute, Oberlin, Western Reserve, and Harvard after 1848, opened their doors to qualified blacks.

Some blacks were even able to acquire substantial property and thriving businesses despite racial barriers. The example of James Forten—only one of many that could be selected—well illustrates this. Forten, a Philadelphia Negro and veteran of the American Revolution, started a small sail-manufacturing shop in the late eighteenth century. By the time of Jackson's presidency, Forten's factory was, in the words of Martin Delany, "one of the principal sail manufacturies, constantly employing a large number of men, black and white, supplying a large number of masters and owners of vessels, with full rigging for their crafts."

When Forten died in the mid-1840's he left a small fortune, though most of his money had been spent in support of the abolitionist movement and in other philanthropic causes.

Charles Lyell happened to be in Philadelphia when Forten's funeral was held. The significance of the event, which he described, pleased him at the promise it suggested for some blacks, but also revealed once again the barriers to full equality that still separated black from white.

A rare event [Lyell wrote], the death of a wealthy man of colour took place during my stay here, and his funeral was attended not only by a crowd of persons of his own race, but also by many highly respectable white merchants, by whom he was held in high esteem. He made his fortune as a sail-maker, and is said to have been worth, at one time, sixty thousand pounds, but to have lost a great part of his riches by lending money with more generosity than prudence. I was rejoicing that his colour had proved no impediment to his rising in the world, and that he had been allowed so much fair play as to succeed in over-topping the majority of his white competitors, when I learnt, on further inquiry, that, after giving an excellent education to his children, he had been made unhappy, by finding they must continue, in spite of all their advantages, to belong to an inferior caste. It appeared that, not long before his death, he had been especially mortified, because two of his sons had been refused a hearing at a public meeting, where they wished to speak on some subject connected with trade which concerned them.

Another career open to northern Negroes but closed to the enslaved blacks of the South was that of abolitionist. In retrospect it is clear that the most important Negroes in pre-Civil War America were those actively engaged in fighting the twin evils, slavery and racism. Men such as Frederick Douglass, Martin Delany, and

David Walker, together with their white allies, were able, in the face of tremendous opposition, to launch one of the most significant reform movements in modern history, aiding both free and bond and leading ultimately to the total collapse of slavery.

6

THE NEW ABOLITIONISTS

It is the duty of the holders of slaves immediately to restore to them their liberty, and to extend to them the full protection of law, as well as its control. It is their duty equitably to restore to them those profits of their labor, which have been wickedly wrested away, especially by giving them that moral and mental instruction—that education, which alone can render any considerable accumulation of property a blessing. It is their duty to employ them as voluntary laborers, on equitable wages. Also, it is the duty of all men to proclaim this doctrine—to urge upon slaveholders immediate emancipation, so long as there is a slave—to agitate the consciences of tyrants, so long as there is a tyrant on the globe.

Elizur Wright, Jr. (1833)

In 1829, the year in which Andrew Jackson took office as the seventh president of the United States, there was published in Boston a short pamphlet with the lengthy title *Walker's Appeal in Four Articles, Together with a Preamble to the Colored Citizens of the World, But in Particular and Very Expressly to Those of the United States*. This pamphlet by David Walker, a free Negro living in Boston, marked the first militant note in the struggle for Negro equality.

Characterizing black Americans as "the most degraded, wretched, and abject set of beings that ever lived since the world began," Walker asked:

Can our condition be any worse?—Can it be more mean and abject? If there are any changes, will they not be for the better, though they may appear for the worst at first? Can they get us any lower? Where can they get us? They are afraid to treat us worse, for they know well, the day when they do it they are gone.

Freedom, Walker contended, was a natural right which Negroes must demand from whites. Though he hoped that this could be gained peacefully, he did not rule out the use of force if necessary. Should violence result, Walker advised his fellow blacks,

make sure work—do not trifle, for they will not trifle with you—they want us for their slaves, and think nothing of murdering us in order to subject us to that wretched condition—therefore, if there is an attempt [at gaining freedom] made by us, kill or be killed.

The main thrust of Walker's pamphlet, however, was not a call to arms as much as a solemn and prophetic warning to all Americans:

Remember, Americans, that we must and shall be free and enlightened as you are, will you wait until we shall, under God, obtain our liberty by the crushing arm of power? Will it not be dreadful for you? I speak Americans for your good. We must and shall be free I say, in spite of you. You may do your best to keep us in wretchedness and misery, to enrich you and your children, but God will deliver us from under you. And wo, wo, will be to you if we have to obtain our freedom by fighting. Throw away your fears and prejudices then, and enlighten us and treat us like men, and we will like you more than we do now hate you, and tell us now no more about colonization [in Africa], for America is as much our country, as it is yours.—Treat us like men, and there is no danger but we will all live in peace and happiness together. For we are not like you, hard hearted, unmerciful, and unforgiving. What a happy country this will be, if the whites will listen. . . . But Americans, I declare to you, while you keep us and our children in bondage, and treat us like brutes, to make us support you and your families, we cannot be your friends. You do not look for it, do you? Treat us then like men, and we will be your friends.

To blacks, *Walker's Appeal* was regarded as "an inspired work." It went through three editions within a year. The author's mysterious disappearance in 1830 only enhanced his reputation as a prophet of the Negro people.

Whites, on the other hand, were vehemently alarmed by "the diabolical Boston pamphlet." Typical of southern reactions to Walker's work was the denunciation of it by the governor of North Carolina who condemned the pamphlet as "an open appeal to their [the slaves'] natural love of liberty . . . and throughout expressing sentiments totally subversive of all subordination in our slaves."

Nor was the alarm and opposition to *Walker's Appeal* limited to proslavery southerners. One of the leading antislavery advocates, Benjamin Lundy, attacked the pamphlet as an "inflammatory" publication. "I can do

All My Trials

Moderate

Hush lit-tle ba - by, don't you cry, _____ You know your Ma-ma _____ was born to die, _____

The river Jordan is muddy and cold,
Well, it chills the body but not the soul,
All my trials, Lord, soon be over,
All my trials, Lord, soon be over.

I've got a little book with pages three,
And every page spells liberty,
All my trials, Lord, soon be over,
All my trials, Lord, soon be over.

If living were a thing that money could buy,
You know the rich would live and the poor would die,
All my trials, Lord, soon be over,
All my trials, Lord, soon be over.

There grows a tree in Paradise,
And the Pilgrims call it the tree of life,
All my trials, Lord, soon be over,
All my trials, Lord, soon be over.

no less," he wrote, "then set the broadest condemnation on it." Even the twenty-five-year-old William Lloyd Garrison, soon to become the best known of the abolitionists, considered this publication "most injudicious," though admitting that it contained "many valuable truths and seasonable warnings."

Two years after the appearance of *Walker's Appeal*, however, Garrison himself was to similarly alarm American whites. Garrison began his lifelong crusade against slavery in 1829 as an assistant editor of the *Genius of Universal Emancipation*—a Baltimore antislavery paper edited by Benjamin Lundy. His activities there soon brought him into conflict with the local authorities, and he was jailed for denouncing the domestic slave trade. Settling in Boston late in 1830, Garrison decided to launch his own antislavery paper, the *Liberator*. The first issue, dated January 1, 1831, struck a new note of militancy in the hitherto moderate white antislavery movement, just as *Walker's Appeal* had done among blacks. "I determined," Garrison announced,

at every hazard, to lift up the standard of emancipation in the eyes of the nation, within sight of Bunker Hill and in the birth place of liberty. That standard is now unfurled; and long may it float, unhurt by the spoilations of time or the missiles of a desperate foe—yea, till every chain be broken, and every bondman set free! Let Southern oppressors tremble—let their Northern apologists tremble—let all the enemies of the persecuted blacks tremble. . . .

Assenting to the "self evident truth" maintained in the American Declaration of Independence, "that all men are created equal, and endowed by their Creator with certain inalienable rights—among which are life, liberty and the pursuit of happiness," I shall strenuously contend for immediate enfranchisement of our slave population.

Garrison realized that his unsparing denunciation of slavery as a moral sin and a violation of basic American principles embodied in the Declaration of Independence would upset many persons—even some who opposed slavery but urged a conciliatory approach. To Garrison there could be no compromise with evil; that evil, slavery, must be removed. Immediate and unconditional abolition was the only solution. In answer to his anticipated critics, Garrison concluded his first *Liberator* editorial with a passionate defense of his tone and tactics:

I am aware, that many object to the severity of my language; but is there not cause for severity? I will be as harsh as truth, and as uncompromising as justice. On this subject, I do not wish to think, or speak, or write, with moderation. No! No! Tell a man whose house is on fire, to give a moderate alarm; tell him to moderately rescue his wife from the hands of the ravisher; tell the mother to gradually extricate her babe from the fire into which it has fallen—but urge me not to use moderation in a cause like the present. I am in earnest—I will not equivocate—I will not excuse—I will not retreat a single inch—AND I WILL BE HEARD.

It is pretended that I am retarding the cause of emancipation by the coarseness of my invective, and the precipitancy of my measures. The charge is not true. On this question my influence—humble as it is—is felt at this moment to a considerable extent, and shall be felt

*in the coming years—not perniciously, but beneficially
—not as a curse, but as a blessing; and posterity will bear
testimony that I was right. . . .*

Good to his word, Garrison continued to edit and
publish the *Liberator* until the last slave was free, some
thirty-five years later. That freedom came at all was due
in no small measure to this dedicated man.

Most of Garrison's white contemporaries, however,
saw racial matters differently. Walker's pamphlet had
been a shock, but, because it was the work of a Negro
and had not been followed up by subsequent writings,
most whites, after the initial furor, forgot it. Garrison's
activities were another matter. Here was a white man
forthrightly demanding Americans to confront their consciences, a man who pointed again and again to the
glaring inconsistencies between America's democratic
ideals and human bondage—between the revered
Declaration of Independence and the institution of
slavery. Furthermore, Garrison's harping on American
guilt was relentless. Not only did his barbed editorials
continue to fill the pages of the *Liberator,* he also organized others to fight for freedom's cause. The same year
that the *Liberator* began, 1831, Garrison helped found
the New England Antislavery Society. Two years later
he drafted the declaration of principles of the American
Antislavery Society—an organization with a growing
membership in New England, New York, and the Ohio
Valley.

As in the case of Walker, Garrison's most dedicated
supporters were Negroes. Of the *Liberator's* first 2,300
subscribers, for instance, 1,725, or three-quarters, were

blacks. Negroes also served as agents in distributing Garrison's paper and were his chief financial backers.

Among white people Garrison was widely hated as a fanatic and a traitor to his race. Interestingly, although the *Liberator* was not allowed to circulate in the South, its contents became known through the common practice of southern newspaper editors reprinting extracts of Garrison's paper in order to denounce it in their own scathing editorials. Because of this, Garrison became infamous throughout the South; a price was even put on his head.

But if Walker and Garrison brought southern tempers to the boiling point, an event in August 1831 caused slaveholders to boil with rage and terror. On the night of August 21 a slave preacher, Nat Turner, a mystic and visionary who believed he was doing God's will, led a band of slaves on a mission of violence in Southampton County, Virginia. Some sixty whites were killed before Turner and his followers were suppressed. The fear of slave insurrections, always present in the South, had become a horrible reality.

Southerners were quick to blame the publications of Walker, Garrison, and other northern abolitionists as the cause of Turner's rebellion, though there was no evidence to this effect. Laws governing slave behavior were made more severe, as were laws for the suppression of antislavery literature. The sense of separation between North and South increased rapidly.

Agitation against slavery was not, of course, new with Walker, Garrison, and Turner. As early as 1700 the Puritan judge, Samuel Sewall of Massachusetts, published a pamphlet, *The Selling of Joseph*, which con-

The discovery of Nat Turner.

demned the legal concept of slaves as property. Organized movements against slavery arose during the era of the Revolution, beginning with the founding of an antislavery society in Philadelphia in 1775. By the 1820s nearly 160 such local organizations were to be found in both the North and the South. Most early abolitionists were religious in outlook, moderate and conciliatory in tone. They favored gradual emancipation with monetary compensation to the slave owners. They did not support coercion of the slaveholders. Nor did they advocate accepting the Negro as an equal. Free blacks were not even allowed to join these organizations. Most members saw the best long-range solution to be the removal of free Negroes from the United States by means of colonization in Africa or some other area of the world.

Such thinking gave rise to the first national organization aimed at an eventual end to slavery, the American Colonization Society. Founded in 1817, with the support of such prominent men as Daniel Webster, Henry Clay, John Marshall, and President James Monroe, the society hoped to persuade slave owners to free their slaves voluntarily. These people would then be deported and colonized in Africa. With the aid of the national government, an area of West Africa was procured. It was named Liberia and its capital Monrovia after the American president.

The American Colonization Society was respectable, popular, and well financed. It was also a total failure. By 1830, after much propaganda and the expenditure of large amounts of money, only about 200 slaves had been freed and sent to Liberia. The increase in the slave population through a high birth rate during these same years was hundreds of times greater.

Furthermore, it became increasingly apparent that the aim of many southern supporters of the society was to rid the country of free blacks, not to end slavery. Also, most colonizationists, northern and southern, felt an antipathy to the Negro, considering him to be "a dangerous and useless element." Very few in the Colonization Society desired to see conditions improved for the free Negro here in America. For instance, when the subject of black education was brought up, a Connecticut colonizationist stated:

Educate him [the black man] and you have added little or nothing to his happiness—you have unfitted him for the society and sympathies of his degraded kindred, and yet you have not procured for him, and cannot procure for him, any admission into the society and sympathy of white men.

Sensing the true motives of the colonizationists, free blacks opposed the movement from the first. At local meetings, state and national conventions, in pamphlets and in newspapers, blacks led the attack against colonization. Typical of the many statements on the subject was this one made at a Negro convention:

This is our home, and this is our country. Beneath its soil lies the bones of our fathers; for it, some of them fought, bled, and died. Here we were born, and here we will die.

Or as the black abolitionist Martin Delany stated more strongly:

NUISANCES " GOING AS " MISSIONARIES," " WITH THEIR OWN CONSENT."

A *page from the* Anti-Slavery Almanac, *1839.*

Martin R. Delaney.

We look upon the American Colonization Society as one of the most arrant enemies of the colored man, ever seeking to discomfit him, and envying him of every privilege that he may enjoy. We believe it to be anti-Christian in its character, and misanthropic in its pretended sympathies.

It was in part the realization that the well-publicized Colonization Society was not really improving the lot of black people, free or slave, which led persons like Garrison to speak out.

Another factor adding to the sense of urgency for Garrison and others was the strong defense of slavery being made by southerners. In the late eighteenth century enlightened individuals generally believed that slavery would prove uneconomical and die out in the South, just as it was doing at that time in the North. But the spread of plantations throughout the lower South in the first decades of the nineteenth century proved profitable and created ever greater demands for slave labor. By the late 1820s, therefore, southerners were more and more reluctant to condemn slavery. Some, in fact, were coming to praise it as a positive good. The following statement made by Governor Stephen Miller of South Carolina in 1829 typified the new southern position:

Slavery is not a national evil; on the contrary, it is a national benefit. The agricultural wealth of the country is found in those states owning slaves, and a great portion of the revenue of the Government is derived from the products of slave labor—Slavery exists in some form everywhere, and it is not of much consequence in a

*philosophical point of view, whether it be voluntary or
involuntary. In a political point of view, involuntary
slavery has the advantage, since all who enjoy political
liberty are then in fact free.*

It is little wonder then that persons who *did* see
slavery as a national evil were alarmed. The new breed
of abolitionists who emerged in the 1830s were determined men and women motivated by moralistic concerns for their fellow man and by the ideals of American
democracy. "We shall spare no exertions nor means to
bring the whole nation to speedy repentance," proclaimed one resolution at the first meeting of the American Antislavery Society in December 1833. They spoke
strongly because, as the black abolitionist, David Ruggles
noted, "the pleas of crying soft and sparing never answered the purpose of reform, and never will."

Beginning with only a few hundred white and black
members in the early 1830s, the new antislavery movement grew rapidly. By the late 1830s there were over
600 abolition societies in Massachusetts, New York, and
Ohio alone. Membership lists reached nearly 200,000 by
1840.

But despite growing numbers it was hard for these
dedicated men and women to win a hearing. As might
be expected, abolitionists were bitterly resented in the
South. In other areas of the country persons were only
slightly less biased against them. Even the United States
government under President Jackson and his successors
aided and encouraged the silencing of antislavery sentiment.

Excluded from the South, harassed by the federal
government, resented by the general public, abolitionists

Mobbing of Garrison in Boston, 1835.

nevertheless continued their crusade, many in the face of violence. Abolitionist meetings were frequently broken up by angry mobs. Lewis Tappan's house in New York City was burned. Rotten eggs and stones were hurled at Theodore Weld in Ohio. Even in Massachusetts, where antislavery sentiment was perhaps most widespread, several incidents of violence occurred. John Greenleaf Whittier, the abolitionist poet, was stoned; the English antislavery advocate George Thompson was nearly killed by an angry mob in Concord.

Garrison's life was threatened repeatedly. In October 1835, when he addressed a meeting of the Massachusetts Female Anti-Slavery Society in Boston, a mob composed of some of the leading citizens was waiting for him. Garrison's own description of this event follows:

> On seeing me, three or four of the rioters, uttering a yell, furiously dragged me to the window, with the intention of hurling me from that height to the ground; but one of them relented, and said—"Don't let us kill him outright." So they drew me back, and coiled a rope about my body—probably to drag me through the streets. I bowed to the mob, and, requesting them to wait patiently until I could descend, went down upon a ladder that was raised for that purpose.

Garrison then managed to escape the mob with the help of "two or three powerful men," though they continued to pursue him. Finally, the mayor threw Garrison into jail allegedly to protect him from further violence. On the walls of his cell Garrison inscribed this statement:

*Burning of Pennsylvania Hall after abolitionists
spoke there.*

Some of the opponents of slavery.

William Lloyd Garrison was put in this cell on Wednesday afternoon, Oct. 21, 1835 to save him from the violence of a "respectable and influential" mob, who sought to destroy him for preaching the abominable and dangerous doctrine that "all men are created equal," and that all oppression is odious in the sight of God. "Hail Columbia!" Cheers for the Autocrat of Russia and the Sultan of Turkey!

▪7▪

LOVEJOY, PHILLIPS, AND DOUGLASS

This struggle may be a moral one, or it may be a physical one, and it may be both moral and physical, but it must be a struggle. Power concedes nothing without a demand. . . . The limits of tyrants are prescribed by the endurance of those whom they oppress. In the light of these ideas, Negroes will be hunted at the North, and held and flogged at the South so long as they submit to those devilish outrages, and make no resistance, either moral or physical. Men may not get all they pay for in this world, but they must certainly pay for all they get. If we ever get free from the oppressions and wrongs heaped upon us, we must pay for their removal. We must do this by labor, by suffering, by sacrifice, and, if needs be, by our lives and the lives of others.

Frederick Douglass (1857)

The worst incident of antiabolitionist violence was the murder of Elijah P. Lovejoy on November 7, 1837. The clergyman-editor of the *St. Louis Observer*, Lovejoy had been forced to flee from Missouri, a slave state, because of his antislavery activities. He moved across the Mississippi River to the "free" state of Illinois, establishing himself in the town of Alton. Twice, angry mobs composed of some of Alton's most respected citizens broke into his printing office and destroyed his presses. The townspeople tried to persuade him to leave. At a general meeting called to discuss the issue, Lovejoy answered them in words that have become a classic defense of free speech:

Why should I flee from Alton? Is not this a free state? . . . Have I not a right to claim the protection of the laws? What more can I have in any other place? . . . You may hang me up, as the mob hung up the individuals of Vicksburgh! You may burn me at the stake, as they did McIntosh at St. Louis, or you may tar and feather me, or throw me into the Mississippi, as you have threatened to do; but you cannot disgrace me. I, and I alone, can disgrace myself; and the deepest of all disgrace would be, at a time like this to deny my Master by forsaking his cause. He died for me; and I were most unworthy to bear his name, should I refuse, if need be, to die for him.

Again, you have been told that I have a family, who are dependent on me; and this has been given as a reason why I should be driven off as gently as possible. It is true . . . I am a husband and a father; and this it is that adds the bitterest ingredient to the cup of sorrow I am called to drink. . . . I know . . . that in this contest I stake not my life only, but that of others also. I do not expect my wife will ever recover the shock received at the awful scenes, through which she was called to pass. . . . And how was it the other night, on my return to my house? I found her driven to the garret, through fear of the mob, who were prowling round my house. And scarcely had I entered the house ere my windows were broken in by brickbats of the mob. . . . I am hunted

Elijah P. Lovejoy.

as a partridge upon the mountains. I am pursued as a felon through your streets; and to the guardian power of the law I look in vain for that protection against violence which even the vilest criminal may claim.

Yet think not that I am unhappy. Think not that I regret the choice that I have made. While all around me is violence and tumult, all is peace within. . . . I have counted the cost, and stand prepared freely to offer up my all in the service of God. . . . I am fully aware of all the sacrifice I make, in here pledging myself to continue this contest to the last. . . . I dare not flee away from Alton. . . . No, sir, the contest has commenced here; and here it must be finished. Before God and you all, I here pledge myself to continue it, if need be, till death.

Present in the audience was Lovejoy's friend, the Reverend Edward Beecher. He was greatly affected by Lovejoy's eloquence. "I could not doubt," Beecher recalled, "that the whole audience was convinced that he was right." Beecher was shocked, however, when a respected townsman

assailed Mr. Lovejoy's character and motives . . . in a style of violent invective, such as I had never heard before. He seemed desirous of lashing the assembly into instant fury; and threatened to proclaim hostility against the abolitionists in all the intercourse of social life; and to sunder all ties which bound them to society.

Dismayed, but not defeated, Lovejoy, Beecher, and other supporters left the meeting. That night they secretly set up a third press which had been brought in by boat up the Mississippi from Saint Louis. Beecher and Lovejoy stood guard that night convinced "that the banner of an unfettered press would soon wave over that mighty stream." Beecher described their feelings:

The morning soon began to dawn; and that morning I shall never forget. Who that has stood on the banks of the mighty stream that then rolled before me can forget the emotions of sublimity that filled his heart, as in imagination he has traced those channels of intercourse opened by it and its branches through the illimitable regions of this Western world? I thought of future ages, and of the countless millions that should dwell on this mighty stream; and that nothing but the truth would make them free. Never did I feel as then the value of the right for which we were contending: thoroughly to investigate and fearlessly to proclaim that truth. . . . I felt that a bloodless battle had been gained for God and for the truth; and that Alton was redeemed from eternal shame. And as all around grew brighter with approaching day, I thought of that still brighter sun, even now dawning on the world, and soon to bathe it with floods of glorious light. Brother Lovejoy, too, was happy.

This sense of joy was ended tragically. The following night Lovejoy was shot five times and killed while trying to defend his third press. Elijah P. Lovejoy became, in Beecher's words, "the first martyr in America to the great principles of freedom of speech and of the press." As Beecher saw it, Lovejoy did not die in vain.

Though dead he still speaketh; and a united world can never silence his voice. Ten thousand presses, had he

The final attack on Lovejoy and his press,
November 7, 1837.

employed them all, could never have done what the simple tale of his death will do.

In the weeks after Lovejoy's murder news of the tragedy spread; the country filled with passion. Many law-abiding citizens, though not abolitionists, were outraged at the violence, particularly since it threatened such basic civil liberties as freedom of speech and freedom of the press. The following statement by congressman and former President John Quincy Adams made after Lovejoy's death well summarized the public outrage over this incident:

That an American citizen, in a state whose Constitution repudiates all slavery, should die a martyr in defence of the freedom of the press is a phenomenon in the history of this Union. It forms an era in the progress of mankind towards universal emancipation. The incidents which preceded and accompanied, and followed the catastrophe of Mr. Lovejoy's death . . . have given a shock as of an earthquake throughout this continent, which will be felt in the most distant region of the earth.

A month after Lovejoy's assassination, a twenty-six-year-old lawyer, Wendell Phillips, sat in Boston's historic Faneuil Hall listening to speeches concerning the event at Alton. After hearing the attorney general of Massachusetts assert that Lovejoy was to blame for the violence and that he had "died as the fool dieth," Phillips sprang to his feet and made his first antislavery speech. His indignant eloquence won him instant recognition as a leader of the abolitionist cause.

The death of Lovejoy had made it clear to Phillips that slavery threatened the freedom of all Americans.

He was particularly disturbed by the lawless power of the mob. He wrote of his own awareness of this power as follows:

A lawyer, bred in all the technical reliance on the safeguards of Saxon liberty, I was puzzled . . . by the fact that, outside of the law and wholly unrecognized in the theory of our institutions, was mob power—an abnormal element which nobody had counted on, in the analysis of the system, and for whose irregular actions no check, no balance, had been provided. The gun which was aimed at the breast of Lovejoy on the banks of the Mississippi brought me to my feet conscious that I stood in the presence of a power whose motto was victory or death.

Phillips came to the conclusion that slavery endured and abolitionists were mobbed largely because a majority of Americans were indifferent to the moral issues involved. He also saw that national politics was but a shallow reflection of majority opinion; one could not trust the politicians to secure basic liberties. It was therefore the necessity of abolitionists to agitate the public mind with enough vehemence to awaken it to the basic moral truths. "The people," he wrote, "must be waked to a new effort, just as the church has to be regenerated in each age."

The role of the reformer, Phillips believed, must be that of the moral agitator. Even if slavery did not exist the need for moral vigilance was ever present. Phillips stated this philosophy beautifully:

Eternal vigilance is the price of liberty: power is ever stealing from the many to the few. The manna of popu-

Wendell Phillips speaking at an antislavery gathering.

lar liberty must be gathered each day, or it is rotten. . . . Only by continual oversight can the democrat in office be prevented from hardening into a despot: only by unintermitted agitation can a people be kept sufficiently awake to principle not to let liberty be smothered in material prosperity. All clouds, it is said, have sunshine behind them, and all evils have some good result; so slavery, by the necessity of its abolition, has saved the freedom of the white race from being melted in luxury or buried beneath the gold of its own success. Never look, therefore, for an age when people can be quiet and safe. At such times despotism, like a shrouding mist, steals over the mirror of Freedom.

The ways in which abolitionists served as "unintermitted" agitators, to use Phillips' phrase, were many. Believing in the rightness of their cause, they planned, in the words of one, "to fight against slavery until Hell freezes and then continue to battle on the ice." Some antislavery advocates used the churches as a forum, harping on the sin of slavery and converting people to antislavery in the name of Christianity. When the churches were closed to them, as was sometimes the case, they spoke from church steps, in fields, on boxes, in hired halls. They demanded a hearing, and, despite disruptions, a hearing they had.

Abolitionists also printed pamphlets and papers, held conventions, petitioned Congress, and entered politics. They did not always agree among themselves, and sometimes the movement seemed to be fragmenting. But this was more a sign of vitality than weakness.

Besides talking and writing abolitionists, there were "running" abolitionists—Negroes who escaped from slavery. Estimates of the number successfully fleeing slavery in the years before the Civil War run anywhere from 40,000 to 100,000. Each one was a direct contradiction of the southern picture of slavery as a benevolent institution which Negroes preferred to freedom. Through swamps and forests, over mountains and by water, many slaves took it upon themselves to gain freedom. Their ingenuity was boundless. Some came wearing wigs and powder disguised as whites. Ellen Craft, a light-skinned mulatto, disguised herself as a southern gentleman and left the South accompanied by her darker-hued husband, William, who played the role of her accompanying slave.

In both the North and the South hundreds of fearless men and women, black and white, served to assist the escaping slave. Informally organized into an intricate network, these persons were the mainstay of the famed Underground Railroad. They provided hideouts, supplies, guides, and other services to the fugitive slave. Though daily breaking the law, risking fine and imprisonment, these persons felt guided by a higher law. As an old antislavery hymn put it:

'Tis the law of God in the human soul.
   'Tis the law in the Word Divine;
It shall live while the earth in its course shall roll,
   It shall live in this soul of mine.
Let the law of the land forge its bonds of wrong,
   I shall help when the self-freed crave;
For the law in my soul, bright, beaming, and strong,
   Bids me succor the fleeing slave.

Not satisfied with individual freedom only, many escaped slaves turned to the antislavery movement to

Ellen and William Craft.

help destroy slavery altogether. By the 1840s former slaves were among the most important of the abolitionists. Personal narratives of their trials under slavery often had a more powerful effect on audiences than the more abstract moralizing of the white speakers.

Many autobiographical accounts of life under slavery were published and had a major impact in the North. William Wells Brown, an escaped slave from Kentucky who became a leading antislavery lecturer and the first Negro American novelist and dramatist, published an autobiography of his life under slavery that went through four editions in less than two years. Frederick Douglass's classic *Narrative of the Life of Frederick Douglass* (1845) became a best seller in both Europe and America, selling more than thirty thousand copies in five years. The success of the most popular antislavery tract of all, Harriet Beecher Stowe's *Uncle Tom's Cabin*, was prepared for by these earlier narratives of runaway slaves.

Brown, Douglass, Henry Highland Garnet, Sojourner Truth, and Samuel Ringgold Ward—all former slaves—became among the most effective lecturers in the abolitionist movement. The most outstanding of these remarkable reformers was Douglass.

Douglass was born a slave in 1817. The first twenty years of his life were passed in bondage. He knew little of his family.

Of my father [he wrote] *I know nothing. Slavery had no recognition of fathers, as none of families. That the mother was a slave was enough for its deadly purpose. By its law the child followed the condition of its mother.*

Though he knew his mother, slavery kept them sep-

Advertisement for Uncle Tom's Cabin.

arated and he saw her only a few times before she died when he was eight or nine.

What he did come to know well was slavery, an institution which he later defined as

perpetual unpaid toil; no marriage, no husband, no wife, no parent, no child; ignorance, brutality, licentiousness; whips, scourges, chains, auctions, jails and separation; an embodiment of all the woes the imagination can conceive.

The harsher aspects of slavery were revealed to Douglass early in life. As a seven-year-old slave working on a plantation of his master, Captain Aaron Anthony, located in the eastern shore of Maryland, he witnessed the brutal lashing of an old black woman. Shortly after this, he saw a cousin of his come to beg protection of the master. She had, in Douglass's words,

been most cruelly abused and beaten by his overseer in Tuckahoe. This overseer, a Mr. Plummer, was, like most of his class, little less than a human brute, and, in addition to his general profligory and repulsive coarseness, he was a miserable drunkard, a man not fit to have the management of a drove of mules. In one of his moments of drunken madness he committed the outrage which brought the young woman in question down to my old master's for protection. The poor girl . . . presented a most pitiable appearance. . . . She had traveled twelve miles, barefooted, barenecked, and bareheaded. Her neck and shoulders were covered with scars, newly made, and not content with marking her neck and shoulders with the cowhide, the cowardly wretch had dealt her a blow on the head with a hickory club, which cut a horrible gash, and left her face literally covered with blood. In this condition the poor young woman came down to implore protection at the hands of my old master.

Expecting the master to "boil over with rage at the revolting deed, and to hear him fill the air with curses upon the brutal Plummer," the young Douglass was shocked when his master ordered the girl back to her torturer. "She deserved every bit of it," the master shouted, and if she did not go home instantly he threatened to "take the remaining skin from her neck and back."

Fortunately, slavery was not all flogging. In 1825 the eight-year-old Frederick was sent to Baltimore to work for Hugh Auld, a relative of Captain Anthony's. Here he served for seven years as a houseboy and later as an unskilled laborer in the shipyards. In this employment he was generally well treated. He even was taught the rudiments of reading by his new master's wife. However, when the master learned of this he forbade his wife to instruct the slave further, proclaiming in front of Douglass: "If you give a nigger an inch he will take an ell [about 45 inches]. Learning will spoil the best nigger in the world. If he learns to read the Bible it will forever unfit him to be a slave."

But Douglass's burning desire for knowledge would not be quenched, and by various ingenious devices he continued his education. With the first fifty cents he earned blacking boots, he bought a school book, *The Columbian Orator*. The more he learned, the more odious did slavery seem to him. He had no answers to the questions that kept springing to his keen mind: "Why am I a slave? Why are some people slaves, and others masters? Was there ever a time when this was not so? How did the relation commence?"

Douglass's worst experiences under slavery were still to come. In the early 1830s Douglass became the property of Thomas Auld, a planter who resided some thirty miles from Baltimore. The rigors of plantation slavery after the relative freedom of the city combined with Douglass's growing general hatred of the slave system made him a very reluctant laborer. In an attempt to make Douglass more docile and obedient, Auld hired him out in 1834 to Edward Covey, a professional slave breaker. For some six months Douglass was overworked, underfed, and flogged regularly. Then one day, out of sheer desperation, he turned on his tormentor and thrashed him. Douglass later recalled this incident as "the turning-point in my life as a slave."

It rekindled in my breast the smouldering embers of liberty. It brought up my Baltimore dreams and revived a sense of my own manhood. I was a changed being after that fight. I was nothing before—I was a man now. It recalled to life my crushed self-respect, and my self-confidence, and inspired me with a renewed determination to be a free man. A man without force is without the essential dignity of humanity. Human nature is so constituted, that it cannot honor a helpless man, though it can pity him, and even this it cannot do long if signs of power do not arise.

From that day forth his life was bent on achieving freedom—first for himself, and later for all blacks. In 1838, Douglass got his opportunity. At that time he was back in Baltimore employed as a calker ·in the ship-

Fugitive slaves escaping from Maryland.

yards. From a free black merchant seaman he borrowed sailor's clothes and an official "protection" paper with an American eagle on it. Boarding a train for Philadelphia, he flashed the eagle-stamped paper whenever questioned. In the late afternoon of September 3, 1838, Frederick Douglass stepped out in Philadelphia a free man: "A new world had opened upon me. . . . I lived more in one day than in a year of my slave life."

He settled in Massachusetts and became active in local antislavery activities. In 1841 he came to the attention of Garrison and was asked to become a lecturer for the Antislavery Society.

Douglass grew quickly as a reformer. A tall, broad-shouldered man of commanding appearance, he was described by a Swedish traveler, Frederika Bremer, as having "an unusually handsome exterior, such as I imagine should belong to an Arab chief. Those beautiful eyes were full of dark fire." Possessed of a deep and melodious speaking voice which by turns could be humorous, sarcastic, sentimental, or indignant, he became an extremely able lecturer. As William Wells Brown, who sometimes shared the speaker's platform with Douglass, once said: "White men and black men had talked against slavery, but none had ever spoken like Frederick Douglass."

At first asked merely to narrate his experiences as a former slave, Douglass was not long satisfied with this. As he wrote:

"Tell your story, Frederick," would whisper my . . . revered friend, William Lloyd Garrison, as I stepped upon the platform. I could not always obey, for I was now reading and thinking. New views of the subject

were presented to my mind. It did not entirely satisfy me to narrate wrongs; I felt like denouncing them.

And denounce them he did—in England, in Ireland, in America. People listened when he defended the black abolitionists in these words:

The man who has suffered the wrong is the man to demand redress—the man STRUCK is the man to CRY OUT—and that he who has endured the cruel pangs of Slavery is the man to advocate Liberty. It is evident that we must be our own representatives and advocates, not exclusively, but peculiarly—not distinct from, but in connection with our white friends.

While delivering the keynote address before a largely white audience celebrating American Independence on the Fourth of July, Douglass asked:

What, to the American slave, is your Fourth of July? I answer; a day that reveals to him, more than all other days in the year, the gross injustice and cruelty to which he is the constant victim. To him, your celebration is a sham; your boasted liberty, an unholy license; your national greatness, swelling vanity; your sounds of rejoicing are empty and heartless; your denunciation of tyrants, brass-fronted impudence; your shouts of liberty and equality, hollow mockery; your prayers and hymns, your sermons and thankgivings, with all your religious parades and solemnity, are to him, mere bombast, fraud, deception, impiety, and hypocrisy—a thin veil to cover up crimes which would disgrace a nation of savages.

Douglass, as David Walker before him, came to believe that freedom necessitated struggle—perhaps even

Frederick Douglass, portrait by J. W. Hurn.

physical violence. Yet he wanted to avoid this and repeatedly warned Americans: "Let us not forget that justice to the Negro is safety to the nation."

Too many Americans *did* forget that simple truth and a civil war resulted—the bloodiest war in this nation's history. But, though the cost was great, the abolitionists had pricked the northern conscience; emancipation came and most abolitionists lived to see all slaves set free. As President Abraham Lincoln stated at the end of the Civil War, only a week before his assassination: "I have only been an instrument. The logic and moral power of Garrison, and the antislavery people of the country and the Army, have done all."

▰8▰

WOMEN'S LIBERATION:
THE BEGINNINGS

*We would have every arbitrary barrier thrown down. We
would have every path laid open to Woman as freely as to
Man. . . . As a friend of the Negro assumes that one man
cannot by right hold another in bondage, so would the friend
of Woman assume that Man cannot by right lay even well-
meant restrictions on Woman.*

Margaret Fuller (1845)

Woman in nineteenth-century America was theoretically
sanctified, but in political and legal matters of reality
she was less than a nonentity. Politically woman had no
rights. Legally she was entitled to very little—in the case
of a wife, certainly not earned money, child custody,
inherited property, or even physical protection: wife-
beating with a so-called reasonable instrument, defined
by a Judge Buller of Massachusetts as a "stick no thicker
than my thumb," was utterly legal.

In some respects the position of white women in
American society was comparable to that of free blacks.
An eminent mid-nineteenth-century jurist, David Dud-

ley Field, summed up the legal status of married women as follows:

A married woman cannot sue for her services, as all she earns legally belongs to the husband, whereas his earnings belong to himself, and the wife legally has no interest in them. Where children have property and both parents are living, the father is the guardian. In the case of the wife's death without a will, the husband is entitled to all her personal property and to a life interest in the whole of her real estate to the entire exclusion of her children, even though this property may have come to her through a former husband and the children of that marriage still be living. If a husband dies without a will, the widow is entitled to one-third of the personal property and to a life interest in one-third only of the real estate. In case a wife be personally injured, either in reputation by slander, or in body by accident, compensation must be recovered in the joint name of herself and her husband, and when recovered it belongs to him. . . . The father may by deed or will appoint a guardian for minor children, who may thus be taken entirely away from the jurisdiction of the mother at his death.

European women who traveled to the United States frequently came with preconceived notions of the democratic nature of American society. They were often shocked at the undemocratic status of women. Harriet Martineau, the English reformer who visited this country in the mid-1830s, came to the conclusion that American women were actually worse off than their European sisters:

The Americans have, in the treatment of women, fallen below, not only their own democratic principles, but the practice of some parts of the Old World. The unconsciousness of both parties as to the injuries suffered by women at the hands of those who hold the power is sufficient proof of the low degree of civilisation in this important particular at which they rest. While woman's intellect is confined, her weaknesses encouraged, and her strength punished, she is told that her lot is cast in the paradise of women: and there is no country in the world where there is so much boasting of the "chivalrous" treatment she enjoys. That is to say—she has the best place in stage-coaches: when there are not chairs enough for everybody, the gentlemen stand: she hears oratorical flourishes on public occasions about wives and home, and apostrophes to women: her husband's hair stands on end at the idea of her working, and he toils to indulge her with money: she has liberty to get her brain turned by religious excitements, that her attention may be diverted from morals, politics, and philosophy; and, especially, her morals are guarded by the strictest observance of propriety in her presence. In short, indulgence is given her as a substitute for justice. Her case differs from that of the slave, as to the principle, just so far as this; that the indulgence is large and universal, instead of petty and capricious. In both cases, justice is denied on no better plea than the right of the strongest. In both cases, the acquiescence of the many, and the burning discontent of the few, of the oppressed, testify, the one to the actual degradation of the class, and the other to its fitness for the enjoyment of human rights.

One major injustice suffered by women was in finding rewarding employment outside the home. In the expanding economy of the Jacksonian era great opportunities for advancement existed. The ambitious go-getter was the nation's social model—the person who could push from log cabin to white house or who could successfully fulfill some other version of the rags-to-riches dream. But this was the masculine model; it was not for women.

In thousands of ways women were told daily that their only proper place was to be married and in the home. "As society is constituted," wrote the author of an 1846 article on the "Domestic and Social Claims on Woman," "the true dignity and beauty of the female character seem to consist in a right understanding and faithful and cheerful performance of social and family duties." The Scriptures were also interpreted to glorify women's domestic role:

> St. Paul knew what was best for women when he advised them to be domestic. . . . There is composure at home; there is something sedative in the duties which home involves. It affords security not only from the world, but from delusions and errors of every kind.

The vast amount of propaganda insisting on women's domesticity was ironic in nineteenth-century America because it came at the very time that numerous women were being forced out of economic necessity into low-paying and degrading factory or domestic work. Margaret Fuller, the brilliant transcendentalist and author of one of the most important feminist tracts, *Women in the Nineteenth Century* (1845), noted this paradox. Women

Hanging Out the Linen Clothes

'Twas on a Mon - day morn - ing, the first I saw my dar - ling A - wash - ing out the lin - en clothes, a -

wash - ing   out   the   lin - en   clothes. ____

Twas on a Tuesday morning, the first I saw my darling
A-hanging out the linen clothes, a-hanging out the linen clothes.

Twas on a Wednesday morning, the first I saw my darling
A-taking in the linen clothes, a-taking in the linen clothes.

Twas on a Thursday morning, the first I saw my darling
An-ironing of the linen clothes, an-ironing of the linen clothes.

Twas on a Friday morning, the first I saw my darling
A-mending of the linen clothes, a-mending of the linen clothes.

Twas on a Saturday morning, the first I saw my darling
A-folding of the linen clothes, a-folding of the linen clothes.

Twas on a Sunday morning, the first I saw my darling
A-wearing of the linen clothes, a-wearing of the linen clothes.

were told that their only proper sphere was the domestic one, yet

thousands and scores of thousands in this country . . . are obliged to maintain themselves alone. . . . Hundreds and thousands must step out of that hallowed domestic sphere, with no choice but to work or steal, or belong to men, not as wives, but as the wretched slaves of sensuality.

The jobs most commonly available to women were in domestic service, textile factories, needlework, and certain other manufactures such as cigar making, shoe making, and printing. Pay for women in such jobs was extremely low, frequently averaging less than a dollar per week, which was far below normal subsistence levels. Of the so-called higher professions, only elementary school teaching was commonly seen as suitable for women—perhaps because teaching younger children could be justified as an extension of woman's domestic role. Female teachers were notoriously underpaid, seldom earning half of the five-dollar weekly wage that the average male common laborer received.

For women who aspired to other professions, the doors were nearly always barred. For example, when a woman applied for a license as captain of a steamboat, the official reaction was that such a license "would shock the sensibilities of humanity" and "would be opposed to the principles which underlie the Christian civilization." Similarly, when Harriot Hunt applied for admission to Harvard Medical School in 1847, she was turned down. Surprisingly, however, the faculty accepted her new application three years later, but the all-male student body blocked her entry, insisting that a woman should not appear "in places where her presence is calculated to destroy our respect for the modesty and delicacy of her sex."

As the case of Harriot Hunt indicates, one of the barriers to the advancement of women was the denial of educational opportunity. With very few exceptions, colleges were closed to women. Men did not prize women who were their intellectual equals. As Margaret Fuller observed:

Much has been written about woman's keeping within her sphere, which is defined as the domestic sphere. . . . It is not generally proposed that she should be sufficiently instructed and developed to understand the pursuits or aims of her future husband; she is not to be a help-mate to him in the way of companionship and counsel, except in the care of his house and children.

Women with intellectual interests were forced to suppress them, especially if married to unintellectual men. One such woman was Jane Grey Swisshelm who eventually became a women's right activist after a miserable twenty-year marriage during which time she kept secret her artistic and literary aspirations. In her autobiography, *Half a Century*, she wrote bitterly of her husband:

I knew from the first that his education had been limited, but thought the defect would be easily remedied as he had good abilities, but I discovered he had no love for books. His spiritual guides derided human learning and depended on inspiration. My knowledge stood in the way of my salvation, and I must be that odious thing—

Margaret Fuller, engraving by E. B. Hall, Jr.

a *superior wife—or stop my progress, for to be and ap-*
pear were the same thing. I must be the mate of the
man I had chosen; and if he would not come to my level,
I must go to his. So I gave up study, and for years did
not read one page in any book save the Bible.

Underlying the inferior position of woman was an
elaborate philosophy which stressed her dependence on
man and her submissive nature. As one writer stated, God
had implanted "the instinct of protection in man and
the instinct of dependence in women." Or as George
Burnap wrote in an 1842 lecture on *The Spheres and
Duties of Women:*

She feels herself weak and timid. She needs a protec-
tor. . . . She asks for wisdom, constancy, firmness,
perseverance, and she is willing to repay it all by the
surrender of the full treasure of her affections. Woman
despises in man everything like herself except a tender
heart. It is enough that she is effeminate and weak; she
does not want another like herself.

It was in this paralyzingly oppressive environment that
the movement for women's rights began in America.
The backgrounds and goals of the early feminists varied
considerably, but one common experience for many female leaders was in the abolitionist movement. Women
in the antislavery crusade learned the tactics of organizing, petitioning, writing, and public speaking, all of
which would serve them well as they turned increasing
attention to their status as women.

Sarah and Angelina Grimké were sisters who had
grown up in a South Carolina slaveholding family. Yet
from their earliest childhood they had hated slavery; as

Sarah M. Grimké.

soon as they were able both women migrated to the North where they joined the Quaker church and the growing ranks of the abolitionists. Having had firsthand experience of slavery, the sisters were invited by the American Antislavery Society to address women's groups on that subject. Their eloquent speeches soon drew widespread attention, and before long men as well as women were crowding into lecture halls to hear the Grimkés.

Such speechmaking was novel in America. Women were not accustomed to addressing mixed audiences. Nor were they expected to do so. Their place, it was assumed, was in the home. Consequently, the Grimkés's public appearances caused great consternation among conservative Americans. Not only were they attacking the institution of slavery which was seen as basic to the nation's economic prosperity and stability, but they were also violating the traditional code of female behavior.

It was not surprising that their lecture tour of New England in 1837 shocked many well-meaning men. The reaction of the Congregational clergymen in Massachusetts was typical. In an official Pastoral Letter from the Council of Congregationalist Ministers, the Grimkés were denounced as unwomanly and un-Christian:

We invite your attention to the dangers which at present seem to threaten the female character with widespread and permanent injury. The appropriate duties and influence of women are clearly stated in the New Testament. Those duties, and that influence are unobtrusive and private, but the sources of mighty power. When the mild, dependent, softening influence upon the sternness of man's opinions is fully exercised, society feels the effect of it in a thousand forms. The power of woman is her dependence, flowing from the consciousness of that weakness which God has given her for her protection. . . . We appreciate the unostentatious prayers of woman in advancing the cause of religion at home and abroad; in Sabbath-schools; in leading religious inquirers to the pastors for instruction; and in all such associated efforts as become the modesty of her sex. . . . But when she assumes the place and tone of man as a public reformer . . . she yields the power which God has given her for her protection, and her character becomes unnatural. If the vine, whose strength and beauty is to lean on the trellis-work and half conceal its cluster, thinks to assume the independence and the overshadowing nature of the elm, it will not only cease to bear fruit, but fall in shame and dishonor into the dust.

The harsh opposition that Sarah and Angelina encountered was a radicalizing experience. They came to see a direct link between the position of slaves and that of women. In 1838 Sarah Grimké directly challenged her critics with the publication of a widely circulated pamphlet on *The Equality of the Sexes and the Condition of Women*. She demanded not only the right to speak out on the slavery issue but also the full equality of the sexes:

God has made no distinction between men and women as moral beings. . . . To me it is perfectly clear that whatsoever it is morally right for a man to do, it is morally right for a woman to do. . . . *It is said woman has a mighty weapon in secret prayer; she has, I acknowledge,* in common with man: *but the woman who prays in sincerity for the regeneration of this guilty world, will accompany her prayers by her labors.* A friend of mine remarked: *"I was sitting in my chamber, weeping over the miseries of the slave, and putting up my prayers for his deliverance from bondage, when in the midst of my meditations it occurred to me that my tears, unaided by effort, could never melt the chain of the slave. I must be up and doing."* She is now an active abolitionist—her prayers and her works go hand in hand.

As women like the Grimkés became increasingly active in the reform movements of the age, the question of the status of women could not help but come to the fore. Not only were women hassled by those hostile to reforms, but even by many males within the reform movements. In 1840, for instance, the American Antislavery Society actually split into rival organizations over the issue of women's rights when William Lloyd Garrison and his followers narrowly elected a woman to the executive committee. Later that same year, at a World's Antislavery Convention in London, the American women delegates, including Lucretia Mott and Elizabeth Cady Stanton, were excluded from participation by a vote which saw the overwhelming majority of male delegates opposed to the women. Both Mott and Stanton took up the cause of women's rights as a direct result of this rebuff.

Lucretia Mott and Elizabeth Cady Stanton helped give purpose and direction to the women's movement. Though it had begun sporadically in the 1830s and early 1840s with petitions, public appearances, and publications such as Sarah Grimké's *Equality of the Sexes* and

Lucretia Mott surrounded by a mob.

Margaret Fuller's *Women of the Nineteenth Century*, the movement did not gain a clear program until the first national Women's Rights Convention held at Seneca Falls, New York, in July 1848. At this historic meeting, which had been organized by Stanton and Mott, a Declaration of Principles that the two women had drafted was adopted. This document was modeled on the Declaration of Independence, but substituted Man for King George III as the tyrant:

> We hold these truths to be self-evident: that all men and women are created equal; that they are endowed by their Creator with certain inalienable rights; that among these are life, liberty, and the pursuit of happiness; that to secure these rights governments are instituted, deriving their just powers from the consent of the governed. Whenever any form of government becomes destructive of these ends, it is the right of those who suffer from it to refuse allegiance to it, and to insist upon the institution of a new government, laying its foundation on such principles, and organizing in such forms, as to them shall seem most likely to effect their safety and happiness. . . . When a long train of abuses and usurpations, pursuing invariably the same object, evinces a design to reduce them under absolute despotism, it is their duty to throw off such government, and to provide new guards for their future security. Such has been the patient sufferance of the women under this government, and such is now the necessity which constrains them to demand the equal station to which they are entitled.
>
> The history of mankind is a history of repeated injuries and usurpations on the part of man toward woman,

having [as its] object the establishment of an absolute tyranny over her. To prove this, let the facts be submitted to a candid world.

There followed a list of some eighteen grievances against Man; some of the most important of which were that:

He has never permitted her to exercise her inalienable right to the elective franchise.

He has compelled her to submit to laws, in the formation of which she has no voice. . . .

He has made her, if married, in the eye of the law, civilly dead.

He has taken from her all right in property, even to the wages she earns. . . .

He has so framed the laws of divorce, as to what shall be the proper causes, and in case of separation, to whom the guardianship of the children shall be given, as to be wholly regardless of the happiness of women—the law, in all cases, going upon the false supposition of the supremacy of man, and giving all power into his hands. . . .

He has monopolized nearly all the profitable employments, and from those she is permitted to follow, she receives but a scanty remuneration. He closes against her all the avenues to wealth and distinction which he considers most honorable to himself. As a teacher of theology, medicine, or law, she is not known.

He has denied her the facilities for obtaining a thorough education, all colleges being closed against her. . . .

He has created a false public sentiment by giving to the world a different code of morals for men and women,

Elizabeth Cady Stanton.

by which moral delinquencies which exclude women from society, are not only tolerated, but deemed of little account in man. . . .

He has endeavored, in every way that he could, to destroy her confidence in her own powers, to lessen her self-respect, and to make her willing to lead a dependent and abject life.

In conclusion the Declaration of Principles proclaimed that

in view of this entire disfranchisement of one-half the people of this country, their social and religious degradation—in view of the unjust laws above mentioned, and because women do feel themselves aggrieved, oppressed, and fraudulently deprived of their most sacred rights, we insist that they have immediate admission to all the rights and privileges which belong to them as citizens of the United States.

The authors of the declaration warned that

in entering upon the great work before us, we anticipate no small amount of misconception, misrepresentation, and ridicule; but we shall use every instrumentality within our power to effect our object. We shall employ agents, circulate tracts, petition the State and National legislatures, and endeavor to enlist the pulpit and the press in our behalf. We hope this Convention will be followed by a series of Conventions embracing every part of the country.

Thus was launched the campaign for women's equality in America that has continued to this day. But unlike the women's movement of the late nineteenth and early twentieth centuries, which concentrated almost solely on suffrage, the pre-Civil War movement, like that of today, was very broad and took many forms. Women realized, as Margaret Fuller stated, that society as a whole would be uplifted if women were.

Improvement in the daughters will best aid in the reformation of the sons of this age. . . . I believe that the development of the one cannot be effected without that of the other. My highest wish is that this truth should be distinctly and rationally apprehended, and the conditions of life and freedom recognized as the same for the daughters and the sons of time.

Women worked to change divorce and property laws, to advance educational opportunities, to gain access to the higher professions, and to win the vote. These were not easy tasks. Many men realized that the feminists threatened the existing social order. As an editor of *Harper's Magazine* wrote of the women's rights movement:

It is avowedly opposed to the most time-honoured propensities of social life; it is opposed to nature; it is opposed to revelation. . . . This unblushing female Socialism defies alike apostles and prophets. In this respect no kindred movement is so decidedly infidel, so rancorously and avowedly anti-biblical. . . . It is equally opposed to nature and the established order of society founded upon it.

Despite such vehemently expressed prejudices, women continued to brave social ridicule in order to gain a larger sphere.

One tack that the feminist movement took was dress reform. "Lady's" dress of the middle period was both uncomfortable and unhealthy. As the abolitionist and women's rights advocate Lydia Maria Child noted in the early 1840s:

The habit of tight lacing, in order to form a slender waist, has been copied, like other European fashions. This practice, combined with the habit of taking very little exercise in the open air, has an unfavorable effect upon the freshness of complexion and beauty of figure.

Fashionable "ladies" wore tightly laced corsets lined with whalebone stays which tended to force the lungs up into the chest cavity, making breathing difficult and fainting common. They also wore several petticoats and long skirts that dragged on the floor or street. In such outfits even physical movement was hard, and an active public life was all but impossible. Men encouraged such female fashions, according to Sarah Grimké, because "they know that so long as we submit to be dressed like dolls, we never can rise to the stations of duty and use-fulness from which they desire to exclude us."

The answer to the problem of dress for women re-formers came to be the "bloomer" costume, consisting of a knee-length dress or skirt worn over loose-fitting pants which were gathered at the ankles. Though named after Amelia Bloomer, who helped to popularize it in her women's rights paper, the *Lily*, the actual designer of the bloomer costume was Elizabeth Smith Miller, a cousin of Elizabeth Cady Stanton and the daughter of abolitionist congressman Gerrit Smith. In her own words, she had

Lydia Maria Child.

adopted the short skirt, after years of annoyance in wearing the long, heavy skirt, and of dissatisfaction with myself for submitting to such bondage. Working in my garden—weeding and transplanting in bedraggled skirts that clung in fettered folds about my feet and ankles, I became desperate and resolved on immediate release. . . . With the short skirt I wore Turkish trousers, but these soon gave place to the straight pantaloon which was much better adapted to walking through the snow drifted roads of my country home.

Other women quickly followed Elizabeth Miller's example, and soon the bloomer outfit became synonymous with female radicalism. Needless to say, ridicule of bloomered women was widespread. As one male college professor warned a young woman who had expressed some interest in the new costume, bloomers are "only one of the many manifestations of that wild spirit of socialism and agrarian radicalism which is at present so rife in our land."

In addition to dress reform, another means that feminist protest adopted was in altering the traditional marriage vows. As early as 1832, when Mary Jane Robinson and the radical labor leader Robert Dale Owen married, they had arranged the simplest ceremony the law would allow.

This ceremony [in their words] involved not the necessity of making promises regarding that over which we have no control, the state of human affections in the distant future, nor of repeating from [sources] we deem offensive, inasmuch as they outrage the principles of human liberty and equality, by conferring rights and

Bloomers, lithograph by Currier and Ives.

imposing duties unequally on the sexes. The ceremony consists of a simply written contract in which we agree to take each other as husband and wife according to the laws of the State of New York, our signatures being attested by those friends who are present.

The most famous feminist wedding in the pre-Civil War era was that of Lucy Stone and Henry Blackwell. Lucy Stone was a graduate of Oberlin, the nation's first coeducational college; both she and Henry Blackwell were lifelong workers for women's rights. When they were married in 1855, they joined hands and read aloud a statement which declared:

While acknowledging our mutual affection by publicly assuming the relationship of husband and wife, yet in justice to ourselves and a great principle, we deem it a duty to declare that this act on our part implies no sanction of, nor promise of voluntary obedience to such of the present laws of marriage, as refuse to recognize the wife as an independent, rational being, while they confer upon the husband an injurious and unnatural superiority, investing him with legal powers which no honorable man would exercise, and which no man should possess. We protest especially against the laws which give to the husband:

1. The custody of the wife's person.
2. The exclusive control and guardianship of their children.
3. The sole ownership of her personal, and use of her real estate, unless previously settled upon her, or placed in the hands of trustees, as in the case of minors, lunatics, and idiots.

Lucy Stone.

4. The absolute right to the product of her industry.
5. Also against laws which give to the widower so much larger and more permanent an interest in the property of his deceased wife, than they give to the widow in that of the deceased husband.
6. Finally, against the whole system by which "the legal existence of the wife is suspended during marriage," so that in most States, she neither has a legal part in the choice of her residence, nor can she make a will, nor sue or be sued in her own name, nor inherit property.

Lucy Stone maintained her maiden name throughout her marriage; women who subsequently have followed this practice are referred to as "Lucy Stoners."

Such changes in the wedding ceremony were important, but largely symbolic. By the time of the Stone-Blackwell marriage, however, the women's movement was beginning to effect more tangible results. In 1848, after extensive petition drives, the New York Legislature passed a Married Women's Property Law, giving women some control over their wages, income, and property. In the years before the Civil War other states followed the New York example.

Several states also liberalized (slightly) their divorce laws during this period. Feminists argued that difficult divorce kept mistreated wives in a state of bondage. As one woman stated:

The law which makes obligatory the rendering of marital rights and compulsory maternity on the part of Woman in the absence of love, and of congeniality, of health, and of fitness, is a deadly despotism; and no woman thus subjected can be pure in soul and body.

The Single Girl

When I was single, dressed up so fine,

Now I am married, go ragged all the time,

Lord, I wish I was a single girl again.

When I was single, my shoes they did screak,
Now I am married, Lord, all they do is leak,
Lord, I wish I was a single girl again.

Three little babies, crying for bread,
Nothing to give them, I'd rather be dead,
Lord, I wish I was a single girl again.

Dishes to wash, and spring to go to,
When you get married, girls, you got it all to do,
Lord, I wish I was a single girl again.

When I was single, I lived at my ease,
Now I am married, have a drunkard to please,
Lord, I wish I was a single girl again!

The efforts of women's rights advocates in the three decades preceding the Civil War also brought some positive, though limited, results in opening up higher education for women. Feminists had to fight the popular assumption that women's constitutions were too delicate to withstand the rigors of Greek, mathematics, and other branches of higher learning. It was commonly asserted, as Sarah Grimké sadly noted, that women were sufficiently "learned" if they knew "chemistry enough to keep the pot boiling, and geography enough to know the location of the different rooms in her house." Such an attitude, she asserted,

is miserable wit and worse philosophy. It exhibits that passion for the gratification of a pampered appetite, which is beneath those who claim to be so far above us, and may justly be placed on a par with the policy of the slaveholder, who says that men will be better slaves, if they are not permitted to learn to read.

In 1821, Emma Willard, who believed that women were the intellectual equals of men, opened a superior secondary school for women, Troy Female Seminary, in Troy, New York. It was there that Elizabeth Cady Stanton had studied as a girl. Mary Lyon, the most famous woman educator of the nineteenth century, founded Mount Holyoke Seminary in South Hadley, Massachusetts, in 1837; this soon became America's first women's college. That same year Oberlin College in Ohio inaugurated the radical policy of coeducation by admitting four women. Though educational opportunities remained limited and often token in the pre-Civil War era, a few other institutions did follow either the Holyoke or Oberlin examples during these years.

Women also made good their right to be heard in public halls. In the antislavery, temperance, and peace movements, as well as in the women's rights crusade, the issue was fought out. Though sometimes silenced and usually heckled, by the 1850s women had generally won the right to speak.

A few determined women also forced their way into previously all-male professions. In 1849, Elizabeth Blackwell became the first woman ordained as a minister.

Such achievements unfortunately were mere tokens. Prejudice and bigotry easily continued to keep most women in a subordinate and dependent state. Some advocates of women's rights became discouraged. One such person was the abolitionist Gerrit Smith. In a letter to his cousin Elizabeth Cady Stanton, Smith observed that:

The object of the "Woman's Rights Movement" is nothing less than to recover the rights of woman—nothing less than to achieve her independence. . . . I rejoice in this object; and my sorrow is, that they, who are intent upon it, are not capable of adjusting themselves to it—not high-souled enough to consent to those changes and sacrifices in themselves, in their positions and relations, essential to the attainment of this vital object.

Stanton in reply to her cousin remained optimistic:

You say you have but little faith in this reform, because the changes we propose are so great, so radical, so comprehensive; whilst they who have commenced the work are so puny, feeble, and undeveloped. The mass of women are developed at least to the point of discontent, and that, in the dawn of this nation, was considered a most dangerous point in the British Parliament, and is now deemed equally so on a Southern plantation. In the human soul, the steps between discontent and action are few and short indeed.

Elizabeth Cady Stanton and her contemporary feminists had taken those first steps from discontent to action. Since that time, many others have followed the course first laid out by these brave women.

HENRY DAVID THOREAU
AT WALDEN POND
An American Alternative

I long ago lost a hound, a bay horse, and a turtledove, and am still on their trail. Many are the travellers I have spoken to concerning them, describing their tracks and what calls they answer to. I have met one or two who had heard the hound, and the tramp of the horse, and even seen the dove disappear behind a cloud, and they seemed as anxious to recover them as if they had lost them themselves.

Henry David Thoreau (1854)

In March 1847 Henry David Thoreau received a letter from a former Harvard classmate asking for information about his life since graduation. It was the class's tenth anniversary and a celebration was being planned. Henry, always reluctant about such affairs, finally sat down in late September of 1847 and answered the letter:

I confess that I have very little class spirit, and have almost forgotten that I ever spent four years at Cambridge. That must have been in a former state of exist-

ence. It is difficult to realize that the old routine is still kept up. However, I will undertake at last to answer your questions as well as I can in spite of a poor memory and a defect of information. . . .

I am not married.

I don't know whether mine is a profession, or a trade, or what not. It is not yet learned, and in every instance has been practised before being studied. The mercantile part of it was begun here by myself alone.

—It is not one but legion, I will give you some of the monster's heads. I am a Schoolmaster—a private Tutor, a Surveyor—a Gardener, a Farmer—a Painter, I mean a House Painter, a Carpenter, a Mason, a Day-Laborer, a Pencil-Maker, a Glass-paper Maker, a Writer, and sometimes a Poetaster. . . .

My present employment is to answer such orders as may be expected from so general an advertisement as the above—that is, if I see fit, which is not always the case, for I have found out a way to live without what is commonly called employment or industry attractive or otherwise. Indeed my steadiest employment, if such it can be called, is to keep myself at the top of my condition, and ready for whatever may turn up in heaven or on earth. For the last two or three years I have lived in Concord woods alone, entirely by myself. . . .

I beg that the class will not consider me an object of charity, and if any of them are in want of pecuniary assistance, and will make known their case to me, I will engage to give them some advice of more worth than money.

Henry David Thoreau was not an ordinary Harvard

graduate. He was his own man. None of the usual professions pursued by educated New Englanders of the time interested him. While others studied law, theology, or medicine, or became businessmen, Henry wandered about the woods and fields in and around his native village of Concord, Massachusetts. As he stated above in answering the questionnaire, he had tried such things as schoolteaching, surveying, farming, and pencil-making. He was good at them, too. But he saw in the lives of his contemporaries an absorption with business and money-making that destroyed a person's true potential.

This world is a place of business. What an infinite bustle! I am awakened almost every night by the panting of the locomotive. It interrupts my dreams. There is no sabbath. It would be glorious to see mankind at leisure for once. It is nothing but work, work, work. I cannot easily buy a blank book to write thoughts in; they are commonly ruled for dollars and cents. . . . If a man is tossed out a window when an infant, or scared out of his wits by the Indians, it is regretted chiefly because he was thus incapacitated for business! I think there is nothing, not even crime, more opposed to poetry, to philosophy, ay, to life itself, than this incessant business.

Thoreau believed that society in its haste to "progress" had lost its sense of values.

If a man walk in the woods for love of them half of each day, he is in danger of being regarded as a loafer; but if he spends his whole day as a speculator, shearing off those woods and making the earth bald before her time, he is esteemed as an industrious and enterprising

Henry David Thoreau.

citizen. *As if a town had no interest in its forest but to cut them down!*

Henry thanked God that "man as yet cannot fly, and lay waste the sky as well as the earth."

The exploitation of nature about which Thoreau complained was, of course, *progress* to most Americans. Cutting down trees cleared land for farming and made money in lumber as well. Money bought more and fancier possessions.

To Thoreau this was all nonsense. "Men labor under a mistake. The better part of the man is soon plowed into the soil for compost." As for possessions, Thoreau had seen too many of his townsmen

whose misfortune it is to have inherited farms, houses, barns, cattle, and farming tools; . . . these are more easily acquired than got rid of. Better if they had been born in a pasture and suckled by a wolf, that they might have seen with clearer eyes what field they were called in to labor. . . . Why should they begin digging their graves as soon as they are born? They have got to live a man's life, pushing all these things before them, and get on as well as they can. How many a poor immortal soul have I met well-nigh crushed and smothered under its load, creeping down the road of life, pushing before it a barn seventy-five feet by forty, . . . and one hundred acres of land, tillage, mowing, pasture, and wood-lot!

Most labor, Thoreau felt, consisted "in throwing stones over a wall and then in throwing them back again." He particularly questioned the technological improvements of the age.

The nation itself, with all its so-called internal improvements, which by the way, are all external and superficial, is just such an unwieldly and overgrown establishment, cluttered with furniture and tripped up by its own traps, ruined by luxury, and heedless expense, by want of calculation and a worthy aim. . . . It lives too fast. Men think that it is essential that the Nation have commerce, and export ice, and talk through a telegraph, and ride thirty miles an hour . . . but whether we live like baboons or like men, is a little uncertain.

The only cure for America's ills, Thoreau thought, would be "in rigid economy, a stern and more Spartan simplicity of life and elevation of purpose."

I am convinced [he once wrote to newspaper editor Horace Greeley] that to maintain one's self on this earth is not a hardship but a pastime, if we will live simply and wisely. . . . It is not necessary that a man should earn his living by the sweat of his brow, unless he sweats easier than I do.

Though Thoreau's belief in the simple life lived close to nature went back at least as far as his college days in the 1830s, it was not until 1845 that he took the opportunity to fully implement his philosophy. In late March of that year, the twenty-seven-year-old Thoreau began construction of a cabin in the woods near the shore of Walden Pond, a small glacial lake about two miles south of Concord village. On land owned by his friend, philosopher Ralph Waldo Emerson, and with an axe borrowed from another philosophical friend, Bronson

Alcott, Thoreau began cutting white pines to frame his new house.

It was a pleasant hillside where I worked, covered with pine woods, through which I looked out on the pond, and a small open field in the woods where pines and hickories were springing up. . . . So I went on for some days cutting and hewing timber, and also studs and rafters, all with my narrow axe. . . . I hewed the main timbers six inches square, most of the studs on two sides only, and the rafters and floor timbers on one side, leaving the rest of the bark on, so that they were just as straight and much stronger than sawed ones. Each stick was carefully mortised or tenoned by its stump, for I had borrowed other tools by this time.

By mid-April Thoreau had the frame and rafters cut and ready to raise. In early May, after having dug a cellar six feet square by seven feet deep, which was later used to store potatoes, Henry invited Emerson, Alcott, Ellery Channing, and other friends and neighbors to help in the raising. This done, Thoreau returned to his solitary work. He completed nailing up the siding and the roofing in May and June, using lumber from a dismantled shanty that he had purchased for $4.25 from an Irish laborer, James Collins. During this same period, Thoreau converted the adjacent briar field into a garden and planted two and a half acres, mostly with beans and potatoes and some corn, peas, and turnips.

Symbolically fitting, he chose July 4, 1845, to move in; this was Independence Day, and Thoreau was asserting his. The cabin was complete except for a fireplace and chimney, which he built in the fall, and plaster on the inside walls which was also added that first fall. The end result was, according to Thoreau

a tight shingled and plastered house, ten feet wide by fifteen long, and eight-feet posts, with a garret and a closet, a large window on each side, two trap-doors, one door at the end, and a brick fireplace opposite.

The total cost of the cabin to Thoreau was exactly $28.12½.

Inside the furnishings were simple, consisting of a bed, a table, a desk, three chairs, a looking-glass three inches in diameter, a pair of tongs and andirons, a kettle, a skillet, and a frying-pan, a dipper, a wash-bowl, two knives and forks, three plates, one cup, one spoon, a jug for oil, a jug for molasses, and a japanned lamp.

The description of Henry's cabin given by his friend Ellery Channing is an excellent one.

It was just large enough for one. . . . It was . . . a sentry-box on the shore, in the wood of Walden, ready to walk into in rain or snow or cold. . . . It was so superior to the common domestic contrivance that I do not associate it with them. By standing on a chair you could reach into the garret, and a corn broom fathomed the depth of the cellar. It had no lock to the door, no curtain to the window, and belonged to nature as much as to man.

Most of Thoreau's time was spent in close communion with nature. He became, in his own words, the "self-appointed inspector of snow-storms and rain-storms . . . surveyor, if not of highways, then of forest paths and all across-lot routes."

He even developed a special ability to communicate with the wildlife. Frederick L. H. Willis recalled a visit he had paid Thoreau at the cabin. Henry had beckoned him outside. Then:

he gave a low curious whistle; immediately a woodchuck came running towards him from a nearby burrow. With varying note, yet still low and strange, a pair of gray squirrels were summoned and approached him fearlessly. With still another note several birds, including two crows, flew towards him, one of the crows nestling upon his shoulder. I remember it was the crow resting close to his head that made the most vivid impression upon me, knowing how fearful of man this bird is. He fed them all from his hand, taking food from his pocket, and petted them gently before our delighted gaze; and then dismissed them by different whistling, always strange and low and short, each little wild thing departing instantly at hearing its special signal.

Thoreau seemed to find at Walden the peace and purpose that escaped him in the money-mad villages of the larger world. The beautiful passage from his journal which follows was written late in the summer of his first year at the pond. It reflects the joy and meaning his life had taken on.

I sometimes walk across a field with unexpected expansion and long-missed content, as if there were a field

Walden Pond.

worthy of me. The usual daily boundaries of life are dispersed, and I see in what field I stand.

When on my way this afternoon, shall I go down this long hill in the rain to fish in the pond? I ask myself. Yes, roam far, grasp life and conquer it, learn much and live. Your fetters are knocked off; you are really free. Stay till late in the night; be unwise and daring. See many men far and near, in their fields and cottages before the sun sets, though as if many more were to be seen. And yet each rencontre [meeting] shall be so satisfactory and simple that no other shall seem possible. Do not repose every night as villagers do. The noble life is continuous and unintermitting. At least, live with a longer radius. Men come home at night only from the next field or street, where their household echoes haunt, and their life pines and is sickly because it breathes its own breath. Their shadows morning and evening reach farther than their daily steps. But come home from far, from ventures and perils, from enterprise and discovery and crusading, with faith and experience and character. Do not rest much. Dismiss prudence, fear, conformity. Remember only what is promised. Make the day light you, and the night hold a candle, though you be falling from heaven to earth "from morn to dewy eve a summer's day."

Why had Thoreau chosen to dwell alone away from society? Two days after he had moved in, he supplied an answer in his journal.

July 6, 1845. I wish to meet the facts of life—the vital facts, which are the phenomena or actuality the gods *meant to show us—face to face, and so I came down here. Life! who knows what it is, what it does? If I am not quite right here, I am less wrong than before; and now let us see what they will have. . . . Even time has a depth, and below its surface the waves do not lapse and roar. I wonder men can be so frivolous almost as to attend to the gross form of negro slavery, there are so many keen and subtle masters who subject us both. . . . One emancipated heart and intellect! It would knock off the fetters from a million slaves.*

Thoreau was not escaping civilization. He merely simplified it. As he wrote in *Walden,* the classic account of his experiment:

I wished to live deliberately, to front only the essential facts of life, and see if I could not learn what it had to teach, and not, when I came to die, discover that I had not lived. I did not wish to live what was not life, living is so dear. . . .

He reduced his dependence on the world to a minimum, building his own house, raising, and foraging, for much of his food, and doing enough additional work to raise money for his immediate needs.

This did not mean the exclusion of society. His house lay near the road, and seldom a day passed when he did not visit town or receive callers at Walden.

Thoreau's new sense of personal freedom made him all the more impatient with the various forms of bondage that men tolerated.

I sometimes wonder that we can be so frivolous, as to attend to the gross but somewhat foreign form of servitude called Negro Slavery, there are so many keen and subtle masters that enslave both North and South. It is hard to have a Southern overseer; it is worse to have a Northern one; but worst of all when you are the slave-driver of yourself.

The individual should be bound by no one, whether the source of that bondage be himself, a group, an institution, or even the state. At Walden, Thoreau worked out these principles. During his stay there an event occurred which dramatized his philosophy and brought him into direct conflict with the state.

One evening late in July of 1846, Henry walked from his pond into Concord to pick up a shoe that he had left at the cobbler's shop. On entering the town, he was approached by Sam Staples, the local constable, jailer, and tax collector. Massachusetts at that time had a poll tax (not a voting tax); each man between the ages of twenty and seventy was required to pay it yearly. Henry, who was never too fond of the state anyway, had not paid this tax for several years. He had not paid it as a protest against slavery and the expansionist policy that had brought the United States into an unjustified war with Mexico. When Staples asked him to pay his tax, Thoreau answered that he had not paid it as a matter of principle and did not intend to pay it now. "Henry, if you don't pay," said Staples, "I shall have to lock you up pretty soon." "As well now as any time, Sam," came the answer. "Well, come along then," replied Staples, and he led Thoreau off to the local jail.

Henry was in jail only one night. Someone, probably his aunt Maria Thoreau, paid his tax, and in the morn-

Central part of Concord, Massachusetts.

ing Mr. Staples released the prisoner. Henry left, picked up his mended shoe, and within a short time was back in the woods picking huckleberries for his dinner.

The whole incident might seem trivial were it not for the fact that it set Thoreau to thinking about the relationship of the individual to the state. From those thoughts emerged his essay "Civil Disobedience"—one of the most powerful and influential statements justifying resistance to unprincipled authority ever produced. In this essay, Thoreau asks: "How does it become a man to behave toward this American government to-day?" He answers "that he cannot without disgrace be associated with it. I cannot for an instant recognize that political organization as *my* government which is the *slave's* government also. . . . This people must cease to hold slaves, and to make war on Mexico, though it cost them their existence as a people."

The problem posed by Thoreau is an age-old one— what is a man of conscience to do when confronted by institutionalized injustice? His answer was both moral and radical. He pleaded for nonviolent resistance.

Under a government which imprisons any unjustly, the true place for a just man is also a prison. . . . A minority is powerless while it conforms to the majority; it is not even a minority then; but it is irresistible when it clogs by its whole weight. If the alternative is to keep all just men in prison, or give up war and slavery, the State will not hesitate which to choose. If a thousand men were not to pay their tax-bills this year, that would not be a violent and bloody measure, as it would be to pay them, and enable the State to commit violence and shed innocent blood. This is, in fact, the definition of a peaceable revolution, if any such is possible.

Thoreau would not be satisfied "until the State comes to recognize the individual as a higher and independent power, from which all its own power and authority are derived, and treats him accordingly."

Published originally in 1849, "Civil Disobedience" at first attracted little attention. Since that time, however, it has influenced the course of world history. Mohandas Gandhi, having read "Civil Disobedience" and *Walden* as a young man, based his successful campaign for Indian independence on the concept of civil resistance. In more recent times thousands of persons throughout the world have continued to find themselves indebted to Thoreau's philosophy of nonviolent resistance to evil. The late Reverend Martin Luther King, Jr., has left the following tribute to Thoreau:

During my early college days I read Thoreau's essay on civil disobedience for the first time. Fascinated by the idea of refusing to cooperate with an evil system, I was so deeply moved that I re-read the work several times. I became convinced then that non-cooperation with evil is as much a moral obligation as is cooperation with good. No other person has been more eloquent and passionate in getting this idea across than Henry David Thoreau. As a result of his writings and personal witness we are the heirs of a legacy of creative protest. It goes without saying that the teachings of Thoreau are alive today, indeed, they are more alive today than ever before. Whether expressed in a sit-in at lunch counters, a freedom ride into Mississippi, a peaceful protest in

Albany, Georgia, a bus boycott in Montgomery, Alabama, it is the outgrowth of Thoreau's insistence that evil must be resisted and no moral man can patiently adjust to injustice.

Nevertheless, although reformers have drawn great strength from Thoreau's thoughts, he himself did not join the reform ranks of his own age. He was never led astray from the belief that reform could only come from within oneself. He refused to become a member of any organization. Institutionalized reform movements were little better than the state.

The true reform can be undertaken any morning before unbarring our doors. It calls no convention. . . . When an individual takes a sincere step, then all the gods attend, and his single deed is sweet.

"Nothing," he wrote on another occasion, "can be effected but by one man. He who wants help wants everything."

Believing this, he returned to his cabin after his night in the Concord jail and continued to live out his individual experiment.

Then, on September 6, 1847, exactly two years, two months, and two days after he had moved in, Thoreau left Walden. As he explained:

I left the woods for as good a reason as I went there. Perhaps it seemed to me that I had several more lives to live, and could not spare any more time for that one. It is remarkable how easily and insensibly we fall into a particular route, and make a beaten track for ourselves. I had not lived there a week before my feet wore a path from my door to the pondside; and though it is five or six years since I trod it, it is still quite distinct.

On his own terms, his life in the woods was a complete success. At Walden he learned a wise approach to life which remained with him the rest of his days.

I learned this, at least, by my experiment: that if one advances confidently in the direction of his dreams, and endeavors to live the life which he has imagined, he will meet with a success unexpected in common hours. He will put some things behind, will pass an invisible boundary; new, universal, and more liberal laws will begin to establish themselves around and within him; or the old laws be expanded, and interpreted in a more liberal sense, and he will live with the license of a higher order of beings. In proportion as he simplifies his life, the laws of the universe will appear less complex, and solitude will not be solitude, nor poverty poverty, nor weakness weakness.

In the bustling, materialistic, expansive, exploitive America of slavery, factories, and the growing power of the state, Henry David Thoreau had found an alternative. His example of moral and physical self-sufficiency remains an inspiration to this day.

-10-

GEORGE RIPLEY AND BROOK FARM
A Second American Alternative

The founders of Brook Farm ought to have this praise, that they have made what all people try to make, an agreeable place to live in. All comers, and the most fastidious, find it the pleasantest of residences.

Ralph Waldo Emerson (1843)

Some twelve miles to the southeast of Thoreau's Walden Pond, in an idyllic setting of gently rolling hills, green meadows, and tall pines, there existed during the 1840s a communal settlement called Brook Farm. The aim of this experimental community was, according to its founder George Ripley,

to insure a more natural union between intellectual and manual labor than now exists; to combine the thinker and the worker, as far as possible, in the same individual; to guarantee the highest mental freedom, by providing all with labor, adapted to their tastes and talents, and securing to them the fruits of their industry; to do away [with] the necessity of menial services, by opening the benefits of education and the profits of labor to all; and thus to prepare a society of liberal, intelligent, and cul-

tivated persons, whose relations with each other would permit a more simple and wholesome life, than can be led amidst the pressure of our competitive institutions.

From its founding in the spring of 1841 until its demise in the late 1840s, Brook Farm was an exciting adventure in living and reform. But before describing the farm, it is important to know something of its remarkable founder and leader, George Ripley.

Born in October 1802 in the western Massachusetts village of Greenfield, Ripley grew up in a respectable and traditionally religious family. Precocious but sickly as a child, Ripley's early life was preoccupied with books, nature, and the Congregationalist church to which he and his family belonged.

In 1819 he entered Harvard College, graduating four years later with the highest academic honors in his class. While a student at Harvard, his conservative religious views were somewhat shaken. For several generations orthodox Calvinism as introduced by the Puritan settlers in the seventeenth century and embodied within the Congregationalist church had been challenged by a growing liberalism. From the early eighteenth century on, a number of theologians came to question such "orthodox" doctrines as human depravity and the predestination of all souls to heaven or hell. Even belief in the Trinity was attacked. By the early nineteenth century it was clear that the Congregationalists were split into two factions. It became common to refer to the liberal members of the church as Unitarians because of their denial of the Trinity.

When Ripley attended college, Harvard and its Divinity School were the intellectual centers of the Unitarian movement, which by then had become a separate church. There Ripley was exposed to a theology that stressed the goodness and rationality of man, and his ability to achieve salvation through good works and Christian living. God was portrayed as a wise and benevolent deity. Such views made a strong impression on the young student, and by his senior year Ripley rejected the orthodoxy of his youth. Accepting the Unitarian creed, he entered Harvard Divinity School and began preparations for a career as a clergyman.

On graduation from the Divinity School in 1826, Ripley was ordained a Unitarian minister and given charge of the Purchase Street Church in Boston. The following year he married Sophia Willard Dana, the daughter of a respected Bostonian, and seemed well launched on a complacent and successful ministerial career.

Two things were to markedly change his life within the next fifteen years and lead him ultimately to establish Brook Farm. First, Ripley gradually accepted transcendental philosophy; second, he came to be increasingly aware of the social, economic, and political ills of the day.

Transcendentalism developed in the 1830s among a group of young Unitarian ministers, including Ripley and his more famous cousin, Ralph Waldo Emerson. Inspired by European intellectuals—especially the German philosopher Immanuel Kant and the English authors Thomas Carlyle and Samuel Taylor Coleridge— these younger Unitarians came to believe that each man had the intuitive power to grasp divine and universal truths. In one of the first published American statements of this philosophy, Ripley wrote in 1836:

There is a class of persons, who desire a reform in the prevailing philosophy of the day. These are called the Transcendentalists—because they believe in an order of truths which transcends the sphere of the external senses. Their leading idea is the supremacy of mind over matter. Hence they maintain that the truth of religion does not depend on tradition, nor on historical facts, but has an unerring witness in the soul. There is a light, they believe, which enlighteneth every man that cometh into the world; there is a faculty in all, the most degraded, the most ignorant, the most obscure, to perceive spiritual truth when distinctly presented; and the ultimate appeal, on all moral questions, is not to a jury of scholars, a hierarchy of divines, or the prescriptions of a creed, but to the common sense of the human race.

This was a radical doctrine since it proclaimed that each individual was responsible for perceiving moral truths. God, Ripley had come to believe, was within everyone, allowing even the most humble and least educated man, woman, or child direct, intuitive knowledge of ultimate truth. Such a philosophy was democratic and antiauthoritarian. It denied to ministers or scholars the special power to interpret God's will; this was the responsibility of each individual. At its core, transcendentalism declared for complete personal freedom. As Ripley wrote, "Man should not live by creeds, forms, or precedents, but freely and spontaneously in accordance with the promptings of his own nature."

This philosophy appealed to an important group of

intellectuals in and around Boston, Cambridge, and Concord. In addition to Ripley and Emerson, there was Margaret Fuller, the women's rightist; Orestes Brownson, the brilliant and caustic critic of emerging capitalism; Bronson Alcott, who would also found a utopian community; Theodore Parker, the most radical of the Unitarian preachers; and Henry David Thoreau. Such intellectuals found in transcendentalism a liberating creed by which they could challenge existing institutions, traditions, and values.

To the conservative and older Unitarians, however, the emergence of the transcendental doctrine appeared as a threat to the basic order and stability of society. As one conservative clergyman charged, when the transcendentalist system

shall have worked out . . . its pernicious and loathsome results; when our young men shall have been taught to despise the wisdom of their elders, and renounce the reverence and submission which the human intellect owes to God; when in the pride and vain glory of their hearts, they shall make bold question of the truths which their fathers have held most dear and sacred; when . . . an undisguised pantheism shall spread its poison through our literature; then shall they who now have stepped forth to introduce this philosophy among us, be held to a heavy responsibility.

During the mid-1830s, Ripley became the focus for the counterattack by conservative Unitarian clergy against transcendental doctrine. Unswayed, Ripley accused his opponents of assuming an elitist role by taking Christianity away from the masses and placing it in the hands of a learned minority. Transcendentalism convinced Ripley that his role as a minister-scholar must be a democratic one. Christian truth, he declared, must always be addressed to "the intuitive preceptions of the common mind."

The second great change that altered George Ripley's life in the 1830s was his growing recognition of man's inhumanity to man. When he became a minister in 1826, the neighborhood of his Purchase Street Church was rather pleasant and respectable. But within a few years the growth of Boston's population combined with the rise of an industrialized working class caused slums to develop around the area. Urban poverty became a very real, daily problem to Ripley. Recognizing this evil, he began to redefine his ministerial role. Instead of dealing with abstract moral issues, Ripley came to believe that the minister must be "hostile to all oppression of man by man. . . . His sympathies are with the downtrodden and the suffering poor."

When the depression struck in 1837, throwing thousands of able-bodied workers out of jobs, Ripley more than ever saw the inequities of competitive capitalism and the class system:

I could not feel that my duty was accomplished while there was one human being . . . held to unrequited labor at the will of another, destitute of the means of education, or doomed to penury, degradation and vice by the misfortune of his birth.

He became increasingly critical of the capitalist system. In 1840 he wrote:

I wish to hear less said to capitalists about a profitable investment of their funds, as if the holy cause of humanity was to be speeded onward by the same force which constructs railroads and ships of war. Rather preach to the rich, "Sell all that you have and give to the poor."

At first Ripley tried to implement his humanitarian ideas through the ministry. His sermons became eloquent pleas "to bring the religion of society into accordance with the religion of Christ." A true Christian church, he stated, should be "a band of brothers who attach no importance whatever to the petty distinctions of birth, rank, wealth, and station."

Although Ripley's congregation listened politely, it was obvious that his words were not changing their lives. Frustrated by this and by the conservative attacks against him, he resigned his ministry in October 1840. He had come to the conclusion that more was needed than preaching. "Such voices," he wrote, "are seldom heard among us—the din of business and politics well nigh drowning all sounds." Nor did he feel that reform could come about through existing political channels. Professional politicians, he believed, inevitably had sordid and narrow objectives.

By the infelicity of their position, they are often compelled to lose sight of the end, in the contemplation of the means, to think only of policy, while they forget humanity. While defending in theory the cardinal principles, that all government is for the good of society and all society for the good of the individual, they neglect to apply them as the practical test of social arrangements.

George Ripley.

No longer expecting that the world could be regenerated by preaching and seeing political parties as poor instruments of change, Ripley in the summer and fall of 1840 hit upon a bold and simple plan for transforming society. He would establish one successful socialist community and it would mark the beginning of the transformation of American society. In November 1840 he wrote to Emerson:

I can imagine no plan which is suited to carry into effect so many divine ideas as this. If wisely executed, it will be a light over this country and this age. If not the sunrise, it will be the morning star. As a practical man, I see clearly that we must have some such arrangement, or all changes less radical will be nugatory. I believe in the divinity of labor. . . . I wish to see a society of educated friends, working, thinking, and living together, with no strife, except that of each to contribute the most to the benefit of all.

Ripley drew up plans to implement his ideal society. In the same letter to Emerson quoted above, he specified how the community would be established:

We propose to take a small tract of land, which under skillful husbandry, uniting the garden and the farm, will be adequate to the subsistence of the families; and to connect with this a school or college, in which the most complete instruction shall be given, from the first rudiments to the highest culture. Our farm would be a place for improving the race of men that lived on it; thought would preside over the operations of labor, and labor would contribute to the expansion of thought; we should have industry without drudgery, and true equality without vulgarity.

An offer has been made to us of a beautiful estate, on very reasonable terms, on the borders of Newton, West Roxbury, and Dedham. I am very familiar with the premises having resided on them a part of last summer, and we might search the country in vain for anything more eligible. Our proposal now is for three or four families to take possession on the first of April next, to attend to the cultivation of the farm and the erection of buildings, to prepare for the coming of as many more in the autumn, and thus to commence the institution in the simplest manner, and with the smallest number, with which it can go into operation at all. It would thus be not less than two or three years, before we should be joined by all who mean to be with us; we should not fall to pieces by our own weight; we should grow up slowly and strong; and the attractiveness of our experiment would win to us all whose society we should want.

To finance his scheme Ripley estimated that about $30,000 would be needed.

We propose to raise this sum by a subscription to a joint stock company, among friends of the institution, the payment of a fixed interest being guaranteed to the subscribers, and the subscription itself secured by the real estate. No man then will be in danger of losing; he will receive as fair an interest as he would from any investment, while at the same time he is contributing towards an institution, in which, while the true use of money is retained, its abuses are done away. The sum *required cannot come from rich capitalists; their instincts would protest against such an application of their coins; it must be obtained from those who sympathize with our ideas, and who are willing to aid their realization with their money, if not by their personal cooperation.*

In accordance with his plan shares were sold, and in April 1841 Ripley, his wife, Sophia, and several others including the novelist Nathaniel Hawthorne settled into the old farm house at Brook Farm. From the start it seemed as if a new life had begun. In May Sophia wrote: "More laughing than of weeping we have had the last few weeks; for a busy and merry household we are at Brook Farm. . . . We feel established and perfectly at home."

In forming his new community Ripley wished to attract members from all classes and backgrounds, but he was especially interested in getting his fellow transcendentalist intellectuals to join. In pursuing this goal, however, it became clear to Ripley that not all transcendentalists agreed with his approach toward reform. While transcendentalist philosophy had led Ripley to advocate an activist and collectivist policy, others—notably Emerson and Thoreau—saw reform as purely an individual matter. Thoreau, after being asked to join the farm, had replied: "As for these communities, I think I had rather keep bachelor's hall in hell than go board in heaven." Similarly, Emerson, after much deliberation, reluctantly wrote to Ripley:

I think that all I shall solidly do, I must do alone. I do not think I should gain anything . . . by a plan of so many parts and which I comprehend so slowly and imperfectly as the proposed Association.

Emerson did add, however, that

The design appears to me so noble and humane, proceeding, as I plainly see, from a manly and expanding heart and mind that it makes me and all men its friends and debtors.

Despite the absence of Thoreau and Emerson, many extraordinary men and women did take up communal living at the farm. As one writer noted there were persons "in most dissimilar external situations—scholars, candidates for the ministry, teachers, mechanics, farmers, young men and young women with no special vocation." Most were enthusiastic about it. By mid-December of the first year, Ripley was able to boast in a letter to Emerson:

We are now in full operation as a family of workers, teachers, and students; we feel the deepest inward convictions that for us our mode of life is the true one, and no attraction would tempt any one of us to exchange it for that which we have quitted lately. A rare Providence seems to have smiled on us in the materials which have been drawn together on this spot; and so many powers are at work with us and for us, that I cannot doubt we are destined to succeed in giving visible expression to some of the laws of social life, that as yet have been kept in the background.

Even Hawthorne, who after leaving Brook Farm wrote a satiric novel—*The Blithedale Romance*—critical of utopian communities, was warmhearted in his initial reaction to farm life. He wrote this description of his activities to his sister:

As the weather precludes all possibility of ploughing, hoeing, sowing, and other such operations, I bethink me that you may have no objection to hear something of my whereabout and whatabout. You are to know then, that I took up my abode here on the 12th [April], in the midst of a snow-storm, which kept us all idle for a day or two. At the first glimpse of fair weather, Mr. Ripley summoned us into the cow-yard, and introduced me to an instrument with four prongs, commonly called a dung-fork. With this tool, I have already assisted to load twenty or thirty carts of manure, and shall take part in loading nearly three hundred more. Besides, I have planted potatoes and peas, cut straw and hay for the cattle, and done various other mighty works. This very morning, I milked three cows; and I milk two or three every night and morning. The weather has been so unfavorable, that we have worked comparatively little in the fields; but, nevertheless, I have gained strength wonderfully—grown quite a giant, in fact—and can do a day's work without the slightest inconvenience. In short, I am transformed into a complete farmer.

This is one of the most beautiful places I ever saw in my life, and as secluded as if it were a hundred miles from any city or village. There are woods, in which we can ramble all day, without meeting anybody. . . . Once in a while we have a transcendental visitor, such as Mr. [Bronson] Alcott; but generally, we pass whole days without seeing a single face, save those of the brethren. . . . The whole fraternity eat together; and such a delec-

table way of life has never been seen on earth, since the days of the early Christians. *We* get up at half-past four, breakfast at half-past six, dine at half-past twelve, and go to bed at nine.

Hawthorne, always a solitary man, later left the farm because, as he wrote, "I have not the sense of perfect seclusion, which has always been essential to my power of producing anything." Yet in afteryears he looked back longingly on the farm and was glad to have "had the good fortune, for a time to be personally connected with it." A passage in the last chapter of *The Blithedale Romance* revealed Hawthorne's feelings:

Often in these years that are darkening around me, I remember our beautiful scheme of a noble and unselfish life, and how fair in that first summer appeared the prospect that it might endure for generations, and be perfected, as the ages rolled by, into the system of a people and a world. Were my former associates now there—were there only three or four of those true-hearted men still laboring in the sun—I sometimes fancy that I should direct my world-weary footsteps thitherward, and entreat them to receive me for old friendship's sake. More and more I feel we struck upon what ought to be a truth. Posterity may dig it up and profit by it.

One of the most important aspects of Brook Farm was its educational system. Here the enthusiasm of the transcendental farmers for creating better institutions was unquestionably successful. Traditional child education in the 1830s and 1840s stressed strict discipline. Students were given materials to memorize and recite; originality or even intelligent questioning was discouraged, and the slightest disobedience frequently led to bodily punishment. At Brook Farm all this was changed. The whole system of education encouraged close relationships between students and their teachers. Not only did they meet together in classes, but also they lived and worked together in close harmony.

Transcendental philosophy taught the divinity of all persons, children as well as adults. When applied to education this meant that children were trusted as being basically good. Consequently, discipline and coercion of students by teachers were virtually eliminated. Classes generally met informally at the convenience of all concerned. In addition students were given a wide range of choice in the subjects they studied. The result was that education became a continuous process based on love, respect, and real communication. One educator described the system as follows:

In education, Brook Farm appears to present greater mental freedom than most institutions. . . . The younger pupils as well as the more advanced students are held, mostly if not wholly, by the power of love. In this particular, Brook Farm is a much improved model for the oft-praised schools of New England. It is time that the imitative and book-learned systems of the latter should be superseded or liberalized by some plan, better calculated to excite originality of thought, and the native energies of the mind. The deeper, kindly sympathies of the heart, too, should not be forgotten; but the germination of these must be despaired of under the rigid hireling system. Hence Brook Farm, with its spontaneous teachers, presents the unusual and cheering condition of a really "free school."

The farm's educational system consisted of an infant school for children under six—the pioneer American kindergarten—a primary school for those between six and ten, and a six-year preparatory program for those going on to college. In addition to classes each student did daily manual labor, enjoyed much time for play, and in general shared in the life of the farm. Many distinguished Bostonians sent their children to the school, and the tuition charged the children of nonmembers became one of the chief sources of income.

Most students thrived at Brook Farm. Their letters reveal their contented situation. The one which follows was written by a young scholar in October 1842. It reflects not only the joys of farm life, but the richness of the cultural and festive activities as well:

My dear Friend— . . . I am still a student, and most of my time has been spent in studies of various sorts; the languages—ancient and modern—attracting me a great deal, but the German and French the most. I do not "burn the midnight oil," and yet I think I am progressing well. Our teachers are all very approachable men and really seem in dead earnest. . . . All the teachers go out of the way to explain points that come up in the lessons.

After hours, we have had many interesting conversations, class readings, dramatic readings, etc., and visitors come who entertain us in various ways. Miss Frances Ostenelli, for one, who has a wonderful soprano voice, and Miss Margaret Fuller from Concord—there is no end to her talk—and also Mr. Emerson from Concord, to whom a good deal pay deference.

Whilst he was here there was a masquerading wood party. . . . It was an open-air masquerade in the pine woods, and the affair was worked up splendidly. . . . The children enjoyed the day much. A large portion of the dresses were home-made. Dances and conversation by the elders filled the day and evening.

Sometimes we have the serious business. Some of the singular persons here affect vagaries and discuss pruderies or church matters, ethics and the like. Or we have some of the Concord people who give us parlor talks. Once in a while they arouse the gifted brothers, and then we have a genuine treat. . . . Subjects relating to a more rational life and education for the poor and unlearned interest me and arouse my enthusiasm. . . .

In long days the sunsets and twilights are delightful and pass pleasantly with a set of us who chum together. I am so near Boston that I go to concerts and lectures with others, or to the theatres, or to the conventions, the antislavery ones being most exciting. In summer I join the hay-makers. In winter we coast, boys and girls, down the steep though not high hills, in the afternoons, or by moonlight, or by the light of the clear sky and the bright stars; or we drive one of the horses for a ride, or we skate on the frozen meadow or brook to the Charles River where its broad surface gives plenty of room.

One thing I like here . . . I have perfect freedom to come or go and to join in and be one with the good people or not. I am not hampered. I go to church or not, as I desire, and I can do anything that does not violate the rules of good breeding.

Even the clothing of the Brook Farmers reflected the freedom and joy they felt. Ripley's community had a flair for living simply, yet beautifully and distinctively; their dress showed this. The men and boys wore large peasant tunics, sack trousers, and heavy leather boots. The tunics were particularly picturesque. As one observer explained:

This favorite garment was sometimes of brown holland, but often blue, and was held in place by a black belt; and for festivals some of the more fortunate youths possessed black velvet tunics. Such an unusual article of raiment excited as much dismay in the outer world as the idiosyncrasies of other reformers, and has been described as a compromise between the blouse of a Paris workman and the peignoir [dressing-gown] of a possible sister.

In addition most of the men sported beards and very long hair—in an age that was relatively clean shaven and shorn. This style was started by Ripley himself.

Women's fashions at the farm were also unusual, gay, and functional. In an era when ordinary women often wore such a combination of corsets, crinolines, stays, and dresses that bodily movement was severely curtailed, the ladies of Ripley's Utopia dressed in short skirts with matching knickers underneath. In addition, noted a resident:

There was a fancy for flowing hair and broad hats; and at the Hive [the main building] dances there might be seen wreaths woven from some of the delicate wild vines and berries found in the woods, twined in waving locks.

Life at the farm was never dull. Between work, schooling, visitors, festivities, and conversations, something was always happening. Surprisingly in this community of so many diverse individuals, personal quarrels were few. They not only lived well together, but also in close harmony with nature. Marianne Dwight, a member of the community noted:

Nature and animal creation here seem to be in advance of humanity. Nothing speaks to me more eloquently of the repose and the love spirit that shall prevail in Association [communal living], than the social state of the animals with us. . . . A gun is never fired here— not a child on the place appears to have the least disposition to molest a bird's nest—and the birds are in consequence surprisingly tame—they do not fear our steps, they come to us to be fed.

By the mid-1840s in competitive, individualistic America, George Ripley felt that he was close to creating his dream of a classless, cooperative Utopia where men, women, and children lived together in harmony and equality. John Codman, first a student and then a member, described the essence of Ripley's Brook Farm dream:

The doctrine they taught above all others was the solidarity of the race. This was ever repeated. It was their religion that the human race was one creation, bound together by indissoluble ties, links stronger than iron and unbreakable. It was one body. It should be of one heart, one brain, one purpose. Whenever one of its members suffered, all suffered. When there was a criminal all had part in his crime; when there was a debauchee, all par-

Brook Farm.

took in his debasement; when there was one diseased, all were afflicted by it; when one was poor, all bore the sting of his poverty. If anyone took shelter behind his possessions, wretchedness, poverty, and disease found him out.

Such was Ripley's dream, and Brook Farm almost realized it. Unfortunately, the community did not survive the 1840s. Several factors brought about its collapse.

The most pressing problem confronting Ripley and the other Brook Farmers from the beginning of their experiment to the end was a lack of capital. The money which supporters of the enterprise had initially invested was sufficient to purchase the farm. It was then planned that the funds brought in through farming, the schools, and other enterprises would cover the operating costs and begin to pay off debts. This was not the case. The soil of the farm proved poor, and most of the vegetables, fruit, and milk produced was consumed by the farmers themselves.

To compensate for the lack of funds from farming, Ripley had established several shops where carpenters, printers, shoemakers, and other craftsmen plied their trades. But these efforts were also disappointing as money-makers. The school remained the chief source of revenue.

The result was that even in the best years Brook Farm was partly dependent on the goodwill of its financial supporters; most available capital was rapidly absorbed in new buildings or other facilities.

In retrospect it appears that another cause of the eventual collapse of the farm came about as the result of a reform in organization. Brook Farm had only been loosely organized when Ripley had first established the community in the spring of 1841. In the fall of the first year some "articles of Association" had been drawn up and democratically agreed to. Later, as Brook Farm became well known because of the glowing published reports of eminent visitors, Ripley and others grew more concerned about articulating the social theories of their community.

During those years utopian communities were being established in various places throughout the country. Many were based on the theories of the French social planner Charles Fourier. Fourier had worked out elaborate schemes for reorganizing society in associations or "phalanxes" of about 1,600 persons. Each phalanx would include every possible employment choice, rendering labor "attractive."

Fourier had never visited the United States, but his ideas were transmitted to American readers in Albert Brisbane's *Social Destiny of Man* (1840) and through the pages of Horace Greeley's *New York Tribune*. Ripley read Brisbane's book even before founding the farm, and Fourier's ideas were often discussed within the community. Both Brisbane and Greeley visited the farm, and gradually Ripley and others came to see in Fourierism a systematic rationale for their long-established values. They also came to believe that if they could make Brook Farm into a model Fourierist phalanx it could serve better as the guiding light for the regeneration of American society. Consequently, in 1844, a new and more elaborate constitution was drawn up and Brook Farm became Brook Farm Phalanx.

This change at first seemed to have little outward

affect on farm life. Looking backward, however, it is clear that the introduction of Fourierism marked a turning point. For one thing, not all members shared the enthusiasm for Fourierism, and a few left the farm because of this.

A second change was the more elaborate organizational schemes adopted. Work was divided more rigidly into "series." There was a ploughing series, a hoeing series, a kitchen series, a washing series, and so on. The result was that some of the spontaneity and individualism of early Brook Farm was lost.

A third change that the introduction of Fourierism brought about was the publication of a national magazine, the *Harbinger*, beginning in 1845. This became the most influential Fourierist publication in the country, and assured Brook Farm the leading role in utopian socialism. However, publication of the *Harbinger* took time away from other pursuits and proved a further financial burden.

Yet despite these somewhat detrimental changes the community appeared to be thriving as a Fourier phalanx. New members were brought in, additional funds were raised, and elaborate plans were made for the construction of a major new building to be called the "phalanstery." For nearly two years, time, energy, and money went into the construction of the phalanstery. The future of the farm was wrapped up in the structure. Confidence rose with the building. By the late winter of 1846, it was nearing completion.

Then, on the evening of March 1, disaster struck. "Fire!", someone yelled, "The phalanstery!" Hastily organized bucket brigades and firefighters from as far away as Boston were unable to stop the blaze. Within an hour and a half the new building was a charred ruin.

The flames consumed more than the phalanstery. They destroyed the dream of Brook Farm as well, though not all at once. Ripley and his associates gamely tried to make a go of it after the catastrophe. But money matters became worse. Various operations were cut back as the farmers, at least those who remained, struggled through a final year and a half. Then, in September 1847, the same month and year that Thoreau left Walden Pond, Brook Farm closed, ending what had been the most helpful and happy of American Utopias.

By the standards of the day neither Brook Farm nor Walden Pond was successful. Both were short-lived and had little lasting influence on the greater society. Yet Ripley, the communalist, and Thoreau, the individualist, were extremely significant. In a money-mad world of exploitation, expansion, violence, sexism, and racism, they offered alternatives. The lessons they taught, of course, differed. But both Ripley and Thoreau spoke for a humane and peaceful world; one free from the curses of materialism, elitism, and war; one lived in harmony with nature. Today in our complex twentieth-century world, such values appear increasingly worthwhile as goals. What Hawthorne wrote of the Brook Farmers applies equally to Thoreau's Walden:

More and more I feel we struck upon what ought to be a truth. Posterity may dig it up and profit by it.

SONG NOTES

All guitar arrangements copyright by John Anthony Scott.

The Wisconsin Emigrant was popular in New England during the Jacksonian period. It expresses well the sharp alternatives that troubled the people of this time: either a life of painful toil and poverty, or a danger-filled hectic race for wealth.

A Paper of Pins is a play song that has been sung for many years in various parts of the United States, and nowhere more than in New England. Lucy Larcom undoubtedly sang it and skipped to it during her childhood.

The Castle of Dromore is a beautiful lullaby that was sung during the Jacksonian era wherever Irish immigrant men and women dug canals, built railroads, or toiled in textile shops.

Across the Western Ocean is a song that was much loved by British immigrants to this country, who came in the first place to dig canals and build the railroads of New England. The beautiful melody to which the song is set was originally a seamen's shanty.

Sold Off to Georgy is a lament and boat song composed by Virginia slaves. It expresses the despair of men and women torn from their families and familiar surroundings, sold to slave drivers, and sent off into the deep South. It illuminates the feelings of hundreds of people kidnapped in the North and sent to share the same bitter fate.

All My Trials is one of the most haunting of the black spirituals that has survived to tell of slavery and enrich our musical heritage. It was sung both in the West Indies and the American South.

Hanging Out the Linen Clothes has been one of the best-loved of American folk songs, especially popular with children. For little girls it eloquently defined woman's role: to be loved by man and to spend the weekdays washing and ironing.

The Single Girl is an equally eloquent married woman's blues from pre-Civil War days.

BIBLIOGRAPHY

This bibliography has been designed for the reference of teachers, students, and school librarians. It includes the main sources used in the preparation of this book, and offers suggestions for further reading on the various topics. All works listed are in print at the time of writing (1973) unless otherwise stated.

General

Bibliographical guides to the literature on Jacksonian America include: Alfred A. Cave, *Jacksonian Democracy and the Historians* (Gainesville, Florida: University of Florida Press, 1964; paperback); Douglas T. Miller, *The Birth of Modern America 1820–50* (New York: Bobbs Merrill, 1970; hardcover and paperback); and Edward Pessen, *Jacksonian America: Society, Personality, and Politics* (Homewood, Ill.: Dorsey Press, 1969; hardcover and paperback).

Useful collections of primary sources and modern commentary on the Jacksonian period include: Douglas T. Miller, ed., *The Nature of Jacksonian America* (New York: John Wiley & Sons, Inc., 1972; hardcover and paperback); Robert V. Remini, ed., *The Age of Jackson* (New York: Harper & Row, 1972; paperback); David Grimsted, ed., *Notions of the Americans: 1820–60* (New York: Brazillier, 1970; hardcover and paperback); Edward Pessen, ed., *New Perspectives on Jacksonian Parties and Politics* (Boston: Allyn & Bacon, 1969; paperback); and Frank

Otto Gatell, ed., *Essays on Jacksonian America* (New York: Holt, Rinehart & Winston, 1970).

There are a number of scholarly interpretations of the Jacksonian era by modern historians. Carl Russell Fish, *The Rise of the Common Man, 1830–50* (New York: The Macmillan Co., 1927; reissued as a Quadrangle paperback, Chicago: 1971) is a social history emphasizing the egalitarian aspects of the age. Arthur M. Schlesinger, *The Age of Jackson* (Boston: Little, Brown & Co., 1945; hardcover and paperback) is a readable interpretation of Jacksonian politics in terms of class conflict. Douglas T. Miller, *The Birth of Modern America* (New York: Bobbs Merrill, 1970; hardcover and paperback) and Edward Pessen, *Jacksonian America: Society, Personality, and Politics* (Homewood, Ill.: Dorsey Press, 1969; hardcover and paperback) stress the growing inequalities of the era, and its antidemocratic aspect.

An appraisal of recent historical writing on the Jacksonian period is given by Lee Benson, "Middle Period Historiography: What is to be done?" in George Athan Billias and Gerald Grob, editors, *American History Retrospect and Prospect*. (New York: The Free Press, 1971; hardcover and paperback).

A Restless Anxious People
The Factories of Lowell
The Tartarus of Maids and Mechanics

Narratives of travelers are among the most valuable sources for the study of the Jacksonian period. Alexis de Tocqueville, *Democracy in America* (1835; reissued as a Vintage paperback, New York: 1954, 2 vols.) is essential reading. See also James Silk Buckingham, *America, Historical, Statistical and Descriptive* (1840; reissued by AMS Press, N.D.); Michel Chevalier, *Society, Manners and Politics in the United States* (1839; reissued as a Cornell University Press Paperback, Ithaca, N.Y.: 1969); Charles Dickens, *American Notes for General Circulation* (1842; reissued as a Penguin paperback, New York: 1972), superficial but interesting reading; Francis J. Grund, *The Ameri-*

cans in *Their Moral Social and Political Relations* (1837; reissued by Kelley, New York: 1970); Thomas Hamilton, *Men and Manners in America* (1833; reissued by Kelley, New York: 1968); Harriet Martineau, *Society in America* (1837; reissued by AMS Press, Inc., New York); Frederick Marryat, *A Diary in America* (1839; reissued by Alfred A. Knopf, New York: 1962, S.W. Jackman, ed.); and Francis M. Trollope, *Domestic Manners of the Americans* (1832; reissued by Alfred A. Knopf in 1949 and as a Vintage paperback, New York: 1964, Donald Smalley, ed.), a carping critique of American life styles which often hits the mark and is fun to read. All the above were European observers. For a selection of impressions primarily by native-born travelers, see Warren S. Tryon, ed., *My Native Land: Life in America 1790–1870* (1952; issued as a Phoenix paperback, Chicago: 1961).

The best general economic history of the era is George Rogers Taylor, *The Transportation Revolution 1815–60* (New York: Holt, Rinehart & Winston, 1951; issued as a Harper Torchbook paperback, New York: 1968). Paul W. Gates, *The Farmer's Age: Agriculture 1815–60* (New York: Holt, Rinehart & Winston, 1960; issued as a Harper Torchbook paperback, New York: 1968) is a detailed study of farming. Two important books treat the intellectual and psychological impact of industrialization: Leo Marx, *The Machine in the Garden* (New York: Oxford University Press, 1964; hardcover and paperback) and Marvin Fisher, *The Workshops in the Wilderness: The European Response to American Industrialization 1830–60* (New York: Oxford University Press, 1967).

The declining status of labor and the rise of a new moneyed elite are the subject of Douglas T. Miller, *Jacksonian Aristocracy: Class and Democracy in New York 1830–60* (New York: Oxford University Press, 1967). The history of Lowell is given in Hannah Josephson's beautifully written *The Golden Threads: New England's Mill Girls and Magnates* (1949; reissued by Russell, New York: 1967). Lucy Larcom's *New England Girlhood* is available in a paperback edition (New York: Corinth Books, 1961). Herman Melville's "Tartarus of Maids" is published in his *Selected Tales and Poems* (New York: Holt, Rine-hart & Winston, 1956; hardcover and paperback).

Parties, Politics, and Democracy

Important interpretations of the politics of the Jacksonian era include: Richard P. McCormick, *The Second American Party System* (Chapel Hill, N.C.: University of North Carolina Press, 1965; hardcover and paperback); Chilton Williamson, *American Suffrage from Property to Democracy 1760–1860* (Princeton, N.J.: Princeton University Press, 1960; hardcover and paperback); Robert V. Remini, *The Election of Andrew Jackson* (Philadelphia: Lippincott, 1963; hardcover and paperback); Glyndon G. Van Deusen, *The Jacksonian Era 1828–48* (New York: Harper and Row, 1959; hardcover and paperback); and Marvin Meyers, *The Jacksonian Persuasion: Politics and Belief* (Stanford, Calif.: Stanford University Press, 1957; hardcover and paperback).

Lee Benson, *The Concept of Jacksonian Democracy: New York a Test Case* (Princeton, N.J.: Princeton University Press, 1961; hardcover and paperback) denies that it is valid to associate the Jacksonians with the advance of democracy. Richard Hofstadter, "Andrew Jackson and the Rise of Liberal Capitalism," chapter 3 of the *American Political Tradition* (New York: Alfred A. Knopf, 1951; issued as a Vintage paperback) presents Jackson and his followers as expectant capitalists looking for the main chance.

Alice Felt Tyler, *Freedom's Ferment: Phases of American Social History from the Colonial Period to the Outbreak of the Civil War* (Minneapolis, Minn.: University of Minnesota Press, 1944; reissued as a Harper Torchbook paperback, 1962) is a fascinating survey of the Jacksonian era's varied reform movements. See also two brief but suggestive studies: Arthur M. Schlesinger, *The American Reformer* (Cambridge, Mass: Harvard University Press, 1950; issued as an Atheneum paperback, 1968), and C.S. Griffin, *The Ferment of Reform* (New York:

T.Y. Crowell, 1967; paperback). David Brion Davis, ed., *Ante-Bellum Reform* (New York: Harper & Row, 1967; hardcover and paperback) is an anthology of scholarly articles. See also David J. Rothman's pathbreaking study, *The Discovery of the Asylum: Social Order and Disorder in the New Republic* (Boston: Little, Brown & Co., 1971; hardcover and paperback).

Jim Crow North
The New Abolitionists
Lovejoy, Phillips, and Douglass

The sources for the study of the antislavery movement are rich; but the general history of this movement still remains to be written. One of the best recent studies is, Aileen S. Kraditor, *Means and Ends in American Abolitionism* (New York: Random House, Inc., 1968; issued as a Vintage paperback in 1968). Louis Filler, *The Crusade Against Slavery 1830–60* (New York: Harper & Row, 1960; hardcover and paperback) is a useful, factual survey with a detailed essay on sources. Other studies that have a degree of usefulness are Dwight Lowell Dumond, *Antislavery Origins of the Civil War in the United States* (Ann Arbor, Mich.: University of Michigan Press, 1936; issued as a paperback by the same publisher in 1959); Gerald Sorin, *Abolitionism, A New Perspective* (New York: Prager Publishers, 1972; hardcover and paperback); and Russel B. Nye, *Fettered Freedom* (Lansing, Mich.: Michigan State University Press, 1949; issued as a paperback by University of Illinois Press, 1972); and Lawrence Lader, *The Bold Brahmins, New England's War Against Slavery 1831–63* (New York: E. P. Dutton, 1961; out of print). An often-quoted older study, Gilbert Barnes, *The Antislavery Impulse* (1933; reissued by Peter Smith, Gloucester, Mass.: 1957 and as a paperback by Harcourt Brace & World, 1964) is heavily biased against the antislavery movement. Leon Litwack, *North of Slavery: The Negro in the Free States 1790–1860* (Chicago: University of Chicago Press, 1961; hardcover and paperback) is a fine study of the status and treatment of black people in northern society. *Black Abolitionists* is the title of a monograph by Benjamin Quarles (New York: Oxford University Press, 1969; hardcover and paperback).

Biographies of antislavery leaders include: Ralph Korngold, *Two Friends of Man* (Boston: Little, Brown & Co., 1950; out of print) dealing with Garrison and Phillips; John Thomas, *The Liberator: William Lloyd Garrison* (Boston: Little, Brown & Co., 1963); Walter M. Merrill, *Against Wind and Tide: A Biography of William Lloyd Garrison* (Cambridge, Mass.: Harvard University Press, 1971); Benjamin Quarles, *Frederick Douglass* (Englewood Cliffs, N.J.: Prentice Hall, 1968; issued as a paperback by Atheneum, 1968); and Milton Meltzer, *Tongue of Flame, The Life of Lydia Maria Child* (New York: Thomas Crowell Co., 1965).

The following important writings by antislavery people have been reissued and are currently available: *David Walker's Appeal* (New York: Hill & Wang, 1965; hardcover and paperback); Edward Beecher, *Narrative of Riots at Alton* (New York: E. P. Dutton, 1965; paperback); Frederick Douglass, *Narrative of the Life of Frederick Douglass* (Cambridge, Mass.: Belknap Press of Harvard University Press, 1960; New American Library, 1968; paperback); and Solomon Northup, *Twelve Years a Slave* (Baton Rouge, La.: University of Louisiana Press, 1968; hardcover and paperback; Dover Publications, 1970 paperback). Charles Mitchell, *Many Thousand Gone: The Ex-Slaves' Account of their Bondage and Freedom* (Bloomington, Ind.: Indiana University Press, 1969; Midland paperback) is an excellent introduction to the many narratives written for or by fugitives from the South.

Women's Liberation

There are a number of recent studies of the history of the women's movement. See especially: Eleanor Flexner, *Century of Struggle* (Cambridge, Mass.: Belknap Press of Harvard University Press, 1957; issued as an Atheneum paperback, 1968); William O'Neill, *Everyone Was Brave* (Chicago: Quadrangle Books,

1969; hardcover and paperback); Robert Riegel; *American Women* (Cranbury, N.J.: Farleigh Dickinson Press, 1970); and Andrew Sinclair, *The Emancipation of American Women* (New York: Harper & Row, 1966; hardcover and paperback). See also Aileen S. Kraditor, ed., *Up From the Pedestal* (Chicago: Quadrangle Books, 1968; hardcover and paperback), an excellent collection of feminist writings, and Perry Miller, ed., *Margaret Fuller: American Romantic* (Ithaca, N.Y.: Cornell University Press, 1970; paperback), which reprints Margaret Fuller's *Women of the 19th Century*.

Henry David Thoreau at Walden Pond

The best introduction to Thoreau is his classic, *Walden*, available in various paperback editions, notably Carl Bode, ed., *The Portable Thoreau* (New York: Viking Press, 1947) which also contains a fine selection of Thoreau's other writings, including *Civil Disobedience*. Henry Seidel Canby, *Thoreau* (Boston: Houghton Mifflin, 1939; issued as a Beacon paperback, 1958) is a detailed and readable biography.

George Ripley and Brook Farm

Fundamental references for the history of the communal movement in the United States are Charles Nordhoff, *The Communistic Societies of the United States* (1875; reissued by Hillary House Publishers, New York: 1960; paperback edition by Schocken Books, 1965) and John Humphrey Noyes, *History of American Socialism* (1870; reissued by Hillary House Publishers, New York: 1961, and as a paperback in 1966). Robert S. Fogarty, ed., *American Utopianism* (Itasca, Ill.: Peacock Publishers, 1972; hardcover and paperback) is a collection of primary sources.

Brook Farm is treated in: Lindsay Swift, *Brook Farm* (New York: Macmillan, 1900; reissued by Corinth Books; hardcover and paperback, 1961), and Edith R. Curtis, *A Season in Utopia* (New York: Nelson, 1961). Henry W. Sams, ed., *Autobiography of Brook Farm* (Englewood Cliffs, N.J.: Prentice Hall,

1958; paperback original) is a readable collection of original sources written by Brook Farm participants. See also Nathaniel Hawthorne, *The Blithedale Romance* (various paperback editions including Norton Library, 1968) and Charles R. Crowe, *George Ripley* (Athens, Ga.: University of Georgia Press, 1967).

ACKNOWLEDGMENTS

Grateful acknowledgment is made for the use of illustrations:

The Edward W.C. Arnold Collection, lent by the Metropolitan Museum of Art, photograph courtesy of the Museum of the City of New York, 11; Yale University Art Gallery, The Mabel Brady Garvan Collection, 90; Library of Congress, 86, 146, 166, 178, 203, 205; Metropolitan Museum of Art, Rogers Fund, 13; The New York Public Library Picture Collection, 15, 63, 99, 117, 119, 149, 155, 156, 160, 163, 175, 188, 190, 194, 201, 220, 224, 236; The Henry Ford Museum, Dearborn, Michigan, 17; American Antiquarian Society, 18–19; New York Historical Society, 24, 31, 46, 93, 114, 153, 169; The Granger Collection, 34, 54, 56, 60, 67, 248; The Bettman Archive, Inc., 38; International Museum of Photography at George Eastman House, 49; Cornell University, Ithaca, New York, 122; Connecticut College Library, 126; New York Public Library, Schomberg Collection, 150; New York Historical Society, Bella C. Landauer Collection, 171; Radcliffe Women's Archives, 197; Concord Public Library, 214.

Grateful acknowledgment is made for permission to reprint copyright material:

University of Massachusetts Press, *Thoreau In Our Season*, John Hicks, ed., © 1962, 226–227; "The Wisconsin Emigrant" from *Country Songs of Vermont* collected by Helen Hartness Flanders, George Schirmer, Inc., © Helen Hartness Flanders.

INDEX

DOUGLAS MILLER teaches history at Michigan State University. His previously published and highly praised *Jacksonian Aristocracy* and *The Birth of Modern America* have contributed to a fresh interpretation of the age of Jackson. Though a Jacksonian specialist, Douglas Miller's research interests are varied. He has published studies on such subjects as William Faulkner, higher education, and the effects of immigration. Currently he is writing a book on the popular culture of the 1950's.

When not teaching, researching, and writing, he enjoys hiking and camping in the Appalachians, or exploring the Maine and Nova Scotia coasts. He plays chess and tennis and likes to ski.

JOHN ANTHONY SCOTT has taught at Columbia and Amherst colleges and from 1951 to 1968 was Chairman of the Department of History at the Fieldston School, New York, where he still teaches. He is also a Professor of Legal History at Rutgers University. Among the numerous books he has authored or edited are *The Ballad of America, Trumpet of a Prophecy,* and *Teaching for a Change.*